# CHINA'S NEW DAWN

# CHINA'S NEW DAWN

## AN ARCHITECTURAL TRANSFORMATION

Layla Dawson

PRESTEL

MUNICH · BERLIN · LONDON · NEW YORK

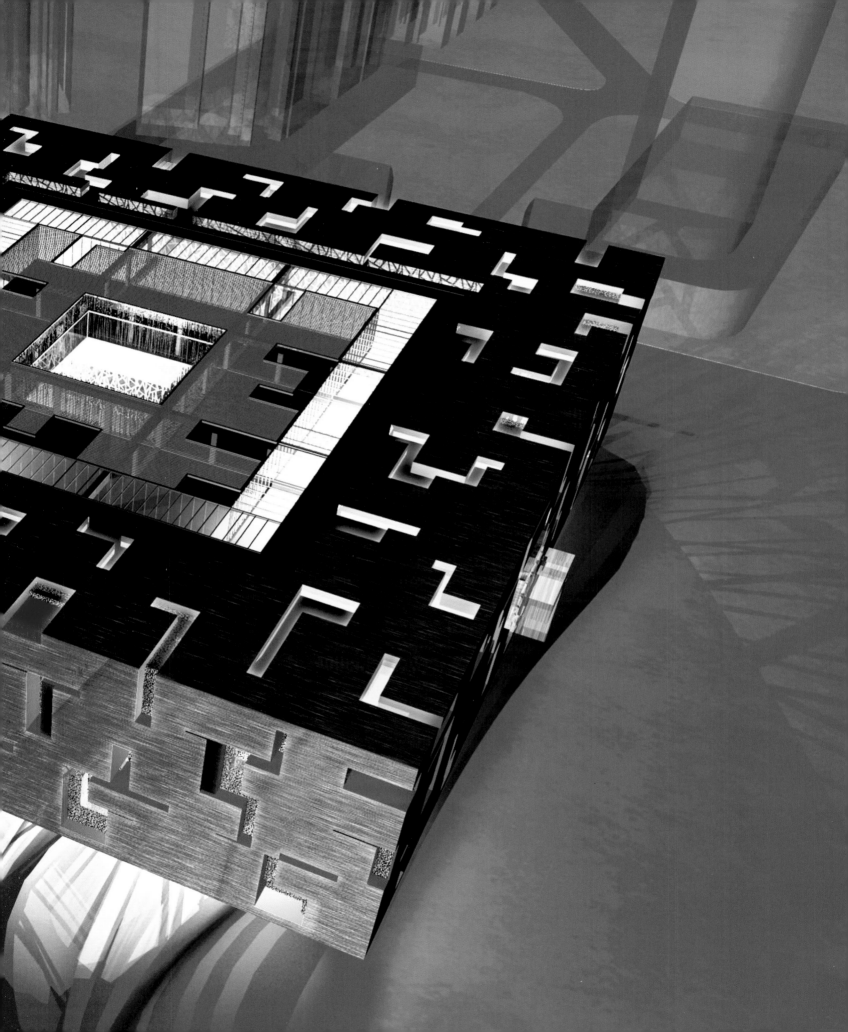

# CONTENTS

# TOWERS TO THE PEOPLE

'Occupy the Chang-an Street and Monopolize the Whole World', is not a new Chinese government foreign policy but a Beijing estate agent's advertising slogan to attract corporate office tenants. The posters, aluminium framed and illuminated in display boxes, have been planted, like soldiers on parade, every few metres along the main boulevard of the capital's newly developing Eastern business district. Construction and traffic noise is ear splitting. The haze hanging in the air, a combination of Gobi Desert sand, coal particles and traffic smog, is like a filmy curtain drawn across the city. The air lacks oxygen and surfaces are coated in dust. Dank and dark spaces under the crumbling concrete and rusting reinforcement of the elevated roads have been cordoned off with wire netting for commuter's bicycles. Executive saloons disappear beneath the office towers into underground car parks. A black Mercedes with tinted windows narrowly misses a passing middle-aged cyclist. The man kicks the car as he wobbles away and shouts a parting insult over his shoulder to the oblivious passengers gliding smoothly down the ramp into their protected car space.

Arriving by train at Guomao underground station, which lies submerged under the China World Trade Centre at the centre of this growing business district, is to step on to the film set of *Blade Runner in Metropolis*. The architecture, all of it designed and built in the last decade, has taken its inspiration from anti-septic polished steel tanks in a Mayan temple landscape. There are blank sloping metal or stone walls without shop windows or any indication of human occupation, building entrances without footpaths, and glazed precipices overlooking roads choked with taxis, cars, buses and intrepid bikers. The one thing Beijing's Imperial and modern architectural styles have in common is their disdain for those at street level. Food vendors, huddling in the available shade, sell steamed corncobs and skewered meat from their three-wheeler stalls to office workers who have bravely ventured out for lunch. Between construction sites men in rags rest on their peddle carts while waiting to be employed as casual transport labour. Between the trees and clipped grass verges,

tended by masked street cleaners and gardeners, beggars bow in supplication for loose change, with their foreheads on the pavement. In the boiling heat of the summer the streets offer no protection from the sun. And, in freezing winter there is no protection from the wind. This is an environment only bearable when viewed from an executive penthouse or air-conditioned limousine.

In Shanghai all the senses are put on high alert from the moment one steps off the plane. Chinese pop music, video clips and digital billboards leave no public space untouched. From Paul Andreu's Pudong International Airport, a steel quilled and glass winged bird hovering over the landscape, the approach into the city on multi-lane highways is accompanied by drivers leaning on their horns rather than their brakes. On a rare clear day, the white and scrubbed Pudong district skyscrapers appear on the horizon like Botticelli's women peaking coyly out of diaphanous shawls and look equally unreal, as though painted on a theatre backdrop. Traffic dives into a tunnel under the Huangpu River and emerges on the West bank in the half abandoned south end of the Bund. Here the concrete and blockwork shells of state factories, with Bauhaus metal-framed ribbon windows and flat roofs, still with their hand-painted gable murals promoting the household goods they once manufactured, are waiting to be demolished. Residents of pitched-roofed, two-storey, timber housing and shop units have already been evicted.

In contrast, the historic Bund's solid parade of Neo-Classical and Art Deco temples have been restored as boutique emporiums, reestablished international banks, luxury-class hotels and restaurants, by the newly empowered middle-class Chinese. For the streets behind the waterfront the early colonialists imported miniature scenes from nineteenth and twentieth-century Europe. Jiangxi Zhong Lu, a unique Shanghai crossroads which is round like a circus, is overlooked by buildings out of the thirties; the Fuzhou building, Metropole Hotel and Development Building by the Davis Brooke Company. All the buildings follow the road line with concave frontages and rise in tiers like Art Deco wedding

**'Occupy the Chang-an Street and Monopolize the World', Beijing property agent's posters**

Tourist esplanade on the Bund, Shanghai

cakes. Side bays peaking to open-arched roof parapets, topped by matching towers, exaggerate the verticality of their inset windows. Despite being the work of different architects, for different clients and functions, they play off against each other in a ping-pong design match, and stand as a cohesive group. Palmer and Turner's Metropole has been reborn as a luxury, modern hotel with the original, worn stone steps leading up to mosaic floored porches and burnished, panelled foyers with deep carpets and chandeliers. Since the 1970s polished black granite and blood-sausage marble utility company offices with heavy, teak, revolving entrance doors, and brick bible society headquarters with brass plates, have been meticulously registered, given plaques to wear and placed under conservation orders.[1] As yet the power and telephone lines, which have not yet been buried underground, hang in neoprene loops between lampposts.

Since the 1980s Chinese visitors have more often turned their back on the Bund to gaze in awe—and swelling national pride—at the new Pudong business spires across the water. An esplanade walk, raised to protect the city from floods, is crowded every day with pensioners and provincial works tour groups, intent on digitally recording that they were really there, posing before the backdrop of a new era and in front of a statue of Mao. One of Pudong's most popular landmarks, sold as a souvenir model in brass, or in snow under glass, is SOM's eighty-eight-storey Jin Mao Tower, which is generally described as an enormous, mutant pagoda. The floors stack up in decreasingly shorter sections. Each section slots into the one below and these artificial joints are visually defined by an upturned trumpet profile, so that the

tower gradually tapers towards the summit's spiky crown and needle antenna. Internally a square racetrack plan encircles an octagonal lift and service core. Fifty levels of office space sit under 555 hotel guest rooms. The adjoining oblong base pavilion, housing conference rooms, is in dragon character. The concave roof, tilting up to acute points at the corners, is a serpent's back. Blank plinth walls at ground level lean inwards as they rise and are pierced only by entrances, under a wavy, glazed awning, and a bull's-eye window. In 2004 Jin Mao was China's highest building. Millions ride the elevators to the eighty-eighth floor sky deck, with its prosaic coffee bar and gift stalls dotted between bright red, raked steel supports, to video the panorama and send greetings from the highest post office in China. The Jin Mao is the quintessential national icon, a good luck symbol because of the number eight theme, a modern copy of a Chinese historical architectural form, and a commercial funfair adventure open to all.[2] Tourists can either gaze in wonder at an instant city under construction or look down into the hollowed out core, lined with the hotel's open corridors, and experience the thrill of vertigo. Giant mirrors reflect daylight downwards into the Grand Hyatt hotel's foyer, thirty-eight floors below. As in all funfairs the architecture is illusory, the pagoda offsets serve no structural need but are purely applied, filigree, metal decoration with patented curtain walling infill. A public jury voted it the best piece of Shanghai architecture and similar to Manhattan's Chrysler Building, another Art Deco tower, it glints by day and glows by night.

Pudong, as it stretches away from the river down Century Boulevard, the Chinese Champs Elysées, is an aggressively bright XXL toy-town, in which pedestrians are overwhelmed by distances and scale. Every destination seems nearer than it is in reality. Crossing the road takes forever. As man made cliffs and mountains Pudong is more impressive as a kaleidoscope of mosaic geometry, spooled past a car window, than as a hands-on experience. From afar, the towers seem to overlap. Up close, they are isolated by wide roads, wide pavements and raised defensive buffers of lawns in granite faced boxes, barriers of clipped hedges, or plants marching in rows. The China Insurance building is a pair of Siamese towers, swaddled in ribbon windows, and sporting two-spoked wheels pierced by hatpins. The Bank of China tower is a lipstick revolving out of its protective sheath and Shanghai Pudong Development Bank has four identical graph-paper façades. Any structure under forty floors is a dwarf in this assembly of royal egos, none of whom are capable of communicating with each other. After hours the lights go out and Pudong ceases to exist. The towers are dormant, the streets empty.

China World Trade Centre, above Guomao underground station, Beijing

Century Boulevard ends at Century Park and the hugely popular, RTKL-designed, Science and Technology Museum. Its architecture has managed to combine a fantasy of the future, with classical Chinese features. Like a more extreme form of Beijing's Imperial Palace and gatehouses, the lofty slabs of the outer wall slope steeply inwards, impregnable except at the official entrance. The crescent building defends itself from surrounding roads by embracing a public but private interior. Within the enclosure, on a round island in a square lake, in turn set in a square garden with four symmetrically placed bridges and entrances, is a walled city of boxes within boxes. The museum is a collection of heavenly bodies. Reflective surfaces enlarge volumes into infinity. In the foyer an auditorium floats in space. The planetarium, a Buckminster Fuller sphere, orbits through a circular cut-out in the roof, and escalators like flying buttresses connect floors. Structural elements branch out at all angles to create an uplifting spirit. Spacious foyers and hangar-like halls are made to seem even larger by the fact that most visitors are children. Wearing school training suits they picnic on plastic mats in the foyer, slide across the polished floors, swarm over the architecture and chatter non-stop. Decibels bouncing off the hard interior surfaces reach deafening levels.

'The Western capitalist powers came one after another and China was thus reduced gradually to a semi-colonial and semi-feudal society'. This is written at the entrance to Shanghai's Museum of the 1921 First National Congress of China's Communist Party in Xintiandi. Translated as 'New Heaven on Earth' this small area, in the former foreign settlement, has been restored for the museum, expensive Eurasian fusion restaurants and elegant shops. In the 1980s Vincent Lo, a Hong Kong property tycoon, formed a joint venture with the Shanghai Communist Youth League. When former League members became municipal government members, Lo was able to persuade them to let his company, Shui On Developments, restyle this central city estate. The dark grey brick, three-storey buildings with ceramic and stone decorative lintels, regularly placed, red-brown painted casement windows, and curly gables, now enclose an open-air handicrafts market and pavement cafes serving espresso and cappuccino to satisfy the Chinese urban fashion for coffee. More rebuilt than conserved, the area has nevertheless set the standard for later historical renovations. The interior of the former French school has been completely gutted to accommodate a dramatically-lit documentation of revolutionary memorabilia, with English and Chinese labels. Visitors in polo shirts and golfing casuals, or grey-haired couples in threadbare suits, clutching

Jin Mao, SOM's mutant pagoda in Pudong

each other for support, spend hours bending over the exhibits, taking great satisfaction in seeing their victory over the colonialists so well presented. The internal defeat of feudalism has been reinterpreted as a national uprising against foreign exploiters rather than a struggle for equality. Outside, the younger generation in designer clothes, exhausted from shopping at Plaza 66 and other glitzy department stores on Nanjing Lu, is drinking and smoking at a Taiwanese restaurant bar. When a stooped old woman dares to beg at their table they make fun of her and a waiter, attracted by the noise, shoos her away, just as the Chinese selling designer scarves are sent packing by Milanese waiters in the Galleria Vittorio Emanuelle.

A train journey into the interior starts at Shanghai Railway Station, designed in 1987 by East China Architectural Design Institute in the International Socialist style, and renovated thirteen years later in the International Hi-Tech style. No one enters the station without a pre-bought ticket and only after having their baggage x-rayed. People gather in one of the fourteen tiled waiting rooms, sitting in rows of plastic bucket seats, until their train has arrived and has been cleaned. Each hall holds a couple of thousand people, families with bulky hand baggage, food supplies and bundles of textiles in striped plastic bags, or business men and women with fashionable suitcases, mobile phones and laptop

From South of the Bund, Foster's Jiushi Headquarters, 2001, ...

**Jin Mao's Art Deco details**

and ionic columns as brash as Las Vegas, together with a large car park, pops up from a cabbage field. A local entrepreneur has built himself a not so mini-Versailles *palais* surrounded by a park of barren earth. His estate is enclosed by wrought iron fencing with carved stone dragons guarding the entrance. More modest family houses, terraced or detached, in every European or American style of suburbia with garages and gardens, spill out of the metropolitan fringes over valuable agricultural land.

These are scenes from China's Eastern seaboard in late 2004, an environment created within only a decade, which has made China the target for business from stagnant Western economies and foreign commentators, who prepotently proclaim Shanghai to be the capital of the twenty-first century. However, the modernization of China began much earlier and throughout the process China's leaders always struggled with the problem of how to deal with foreign cultures. Insularity and rejection, or open borders allowing adaptation and absorption? The latter policy risked the loss of 'Chinese-ness', and gave rise to sporadic resistance, sometimes retreating into xenophobia.

Modernization has arrived in violent fits and starts, so much so that a Chinese friend recently wondered if it had been worth a world war, civil war and three revolutions to return to a point the more developed East coast cities had already reached by the 1930s. In a roll back of history, firms like South-East Asia's P&T Group, founded in Shanghai, or the Pei family of architects, father and sons, whose history is inextricably linked with that of the Bank of China, are returning.

### IMPORTED CHANGE

Despite a history of 5,000 years in which the Chinese invented paper, paper currency, credit banking, the travel compass and gunpowder, western style modernization came only about through outside military force. Before 1842 the sheer size of the largest nation on earth, 9.6 million square kilometres, with encircling oceans and mountain ranges, and the continuity of a centralized state encouraged an insular mentality.[4] Increasingly, however, China's feudal and Imperial dynasties were having to deal with the 'barbarians' outside the Middle Kingdom, Jesuits bent on saving souls and winning spheres of influence, and traders wanting to open up the interior for earthly profit. It was an unequal battle. The superstitions of the illiterate Chinese were matched only by the ignorance of their rulers, the majority of whom knew nothing of science. The foreigners had more effective weapons, industrial tools, technical education, commercial management and transport methods. Eventually, in 1842, the

computer bags. Tickets are checked again before passengers proceed to the platform, where wagon attendants in smart uniforms and white gloves make a final ticket check, before allowing passengers to board and find their reserved, 'hard' or 'soft' class, seats. Mass management methods sometimes only reinforce China's authoritarian image.

During the first hour of the journey a dense forest of towers, apartments topped with domes, pergolas and Greek columns, enmeshed in a spaghetti of roadways, flash past. Although clad in different stone, painted different colours, with or without balconies, awnings and bays, together they form one indistinguishable, blurred wallpaper. Shanghai's generous tax allowances for house financing have resulted in a property investment boom.[3] In Hangzhou, housing prices rose 50% in just two years between 2002 and 2004. Wives of the newly rich organize coach parties to go on apartment-buying sprees, instead of stashing their money in bank vaults. Many flats remain unoccupied, while those who need housing are priced out of the market. An hour away from the city, the buildings thin out and shrink in height. Factories, steel-framed sheds and pre-cast concrete assemblies have been scattered among rice paddies, fruit orchards and market gardens. A casino with an illuminated sign larger than its façade, a top-heavy plaster frieze with a Greek key pattern

**... to North of the Bund, P&T's Peace Hotel, 1928**

'foreign devils' and 'long noses' forced China to relinquish Hong Kong and five other Treaty Ports for the establishment of commercial interfaces between Chinese and non-Chinese on the coastal fringes of the Middle Kingdom, far away from the Imperial Court in Beijing. Foreigners congratulated themselves on having wrested these territorial rights from the Emperor but the Chinese succeeded in trimming foreign ambitions by a strategy of 'divide and rule'. For example, the national railway network was parcelled out to different nationalities, a method still used today by Chinese clients who pit foreign building professionals and manufacturers against each other to avoid creating dependencies.

While the foreigners were kept at arms length, Beijing, planned in 1406 as a model city according to the Han era book

The monumental post-1949 People's Palace

of etiquette, remained square, walled and on an axis of cardinal points, with its most important façade and entrances facing south. In the Forbidden Imperial City the opposing elements of Yin and Yang, created by means of artificial hills and lakes, were weighed against each other to induce harmony and pacify Nature's demons. Grids of clan houses, built around courtyards, and cobbled lanes evolved continuously from 1206 until 1908, during the Yuan, Ming and Qing dynasties, fanned out from the Forbidden City walls. The further away the lower the status of the residents. Hand-workers employed by the court lived closest to their patrons. The visual difference between the elevated Imperial structures and low-level citizens' housing did not change post

1949. New state architecture was 'for the people' but still looked down on them. Beijing had to wait until Paul Andreu's National Theatre in 2004 for architecture created at the people's level.

In the depths of the provinces other walled cities built to the same pattern remained unaffected by foreign influence and a curious form of clan housing, 'Tulou', still exists in Fujian province.[5] Constructed by the Hakka people who migrated south from Northern China in 900 A.D., these unique settlements consist of circular or oval family houses, up to five storeys high, with unroofed courtyards in the centre. Rooms on the upper levels open out on to a continuous balcony encircling and over-looking the courtyard below. From the terraced hills above the villages the pitched clay tiled roofs look like terracotta doughnuts. Frame and roof structures are timber; walls are clay wattle and daub. This is an earthquake zone and the remaining 'Tulou', although intact and still inhabited, are fragile. So far, the oldest discovered element is a 700-year-old beam. Each 'Tulou' has three doorways, the main south door for People, the eastern door of Heaven, and the western-facing Earth door. There is never a door on the north façade as this is the direction in which money disappears.

The first western, imported architecture was built in the 1842 Treaty Ports, which became the seedbeds for China's modernization.[6] These isolated European settlements on Chinese soil were individually shaped by whichever foreign power was in command. To this day German building regulations still apply in Qingdao, where an Anglo-German company began brewing 'Tsingtao' beer, now exported worldwide. Qingdao was first occupied by the German navy in 1897 when the colonial administration razed all Chinese villages to the ground—apart from a temple and the Chinese General's residence. They constructed a 'home from home', built according to German standards for Europeans, and a new village, Taitungchen, for Chinese who had been made homeless. The building contractor for many of the principal buildings was F.H. Schmidt of Hamburg. The architects were German and designed accordingly in Jugendstil and Neo-Romanesque with hipped, red-tiled roofs, rustic granite plinths and corners with plastered walls, sometimes with half-timbered upper storeys.[7] Likewise in Shanghai, foreign traders formed the first municipal authority to impose taxes to pay for town planning, street lights and a private police force, not in the interests of the Chinese inhabitants but to protect their own investments.[8] All over China the standard British trading head-quarters were adapted from a colonial 'bungalow' type brought from India. Called a 'Hong', it was a walled compound of housing

'Little Europe', the Huangpu District behind the Bund

and offices, with perimeter verandahs, kitchen and servants buildings connected by covered walkways, 'go-downs' (warehouses), and 'mafoo' (grooms) quarters. The design served a sub-tropical climate but had nothing to do with Chinese traditional architecture. Plans were drawn up by the merchants with help from a Chinese builder, and construction was managed by the foreign merchant's 'comprador'.[9] The result was the 'compradoric' architectural style.[10] Even the Austro-Hungarian Empire left architectural traces in China, although they governed the northern port of Tianjin for only fifteen years, from 1902 to 1917.[11]

## THEM AND US

China's second 'modernization' took place after the fall of the Imperial Court and the founding of the Republic of China in 1911 with Sun Yat-sen as the first President. A nationalist semi-democratic government was formed by Chinese who had studied in the West but the feudal structure, from which the new elite derived their income, was still in place. Sun Yat-sen's villa on Xiangshan Lu, in Shanghai's French Concession, where he and his wife met with nationalist reformers and communist leaders from 1918 to 1924, has stuccoed façades, side-opening casement windows, wallpaper and dados, polished floors, glass-fronted, American-style bookcases, heavy dark wood occasional tables and a solid matrimonial bed, surrounded by family photographs and pictures of cats. It could be a detached family house in a respectable middle-class English town of the same era.[12] Chou Enlai's house nearby is also uncompromisingly staid and suburban, with an enclosed garden of shrubs and trees around a lawn, but inside the bare waxed floorboards, distempered walls and curtainless windows, with camp beds and office tables for typewriters is more like a Chinese scholars retreat for study and calligraphy. Photographs, however, show Chou Enlai and comrades, wearing western suits complete with Homburg hats, travelling to meetings in an American car donated by supporters.

In 1938, walking up a tidy path between playing fields, college buildings and villa gardens, in Paak Hok Tung, an American and English missionary village near Guangzhou, the English tourists W. H. Auden and Christopher Isherwood imagined themselves "… at home in one of the pleasanter London suburbs." At Hangzhou's Racing Club, frequented by both Europeans and rich Chinese who were keen gamblers and racehorse owners, Auden remarked that they might as well be in the heart of Surrey because "… all trace of China has been lovingly obliterated."[13] Then, as now, China's ruling class had a foot in both the East and the West. They adopted a patina of American and European attitudes, and existed in a social vacuum, enjoying western household conveniences, foreign travel, western education and entertainment, far removed from the poverty of the peasants and servants who enjoyed no universal franchise. Chinese traders and manufacturers sent their sons, and very rarely daughters, to study in Europe, America and Japan. Everything from western or westernised countries was considered technologically and scientifically advanced; while most women stayed at home and were westernised by proxy, through magazines and advertising, European fashion and architecture, a small but influential number of young men were sent abroad to obtain a university education not obtainable in China.[14]

One of the few women sent to the West was Lin Huyin. Her father, Lin Changmin, was a diplomat in London. She wanted to

**Paul Andreu's National Theatre nearing completion, 2004, Beijing**

study architecture, like her prospective husband Liang Sicheng, at Pennsylvania University but the Americans did not think women should take up a man's profession and she had to choose Fine Art instead. During the thirties the couple documented China's historical architecture. Shortly after 1949, when the People's Republic of China was remodelling the capital, Liang Sichang suggested a new people's park, incorporating Beijing's old city walls, but a younger generation of planners found their existence a hindrance to modern traffic flow, as well as politically incorrect, and rejected Liang's suggestion as impractical and feudal. The walls were demolished to make way for the present freeway boulevards.[15]

**Pudong skyline from across the Huangpu River**

Lu Qianschou's Bank of China, 1936

By 1931 returning architecture graduates had begun to take business into their own hands and the China Architects Academy had thirty-nine members, of whom twenty-nine had studied in the USA. Of the thirty registered architects offices in 1936 more than a third were Chinese. The styles in which they designed were all imported and most of the new architecture was in Shanghai, the city with the most international population of Indians, Russians, refugee European Jews, Japanese, Europeans and Americans. Broadway Mansions, a brick patterned Art Deco apartment block, at the North end of the Bund beside the Wusong River, would not have looked out of place in Manhattan. The municipal market hall on Fuzhou Road appeared in the Bauhaus style. Buildings for twentieth-century functions tended to take inspiration from Art Nouveau, Expressionism and Cubism, while conservative functions, trading and banking, went in for conservative Neo-Classical symmetry and ornamentation. Lu Qianshou, while working at Palmer & Turner, designed the 1936 Bank of China on the Bund as a hierarchical, rising, Egyptian stele, with symmetry and an attic storey, classical Chinese lifted eaves, a carved frieze under the roofline and Chinese fretwork panels cut into the stone façade. Shanghai's 1916 Labour Union building, with a pinnacle of Greek Corinthian columns topped with a minaret turban on one of the Bund intersections, was

designed by Guo Yanmo, another Palmer & Turner architect. Of the surviving Bund buildings 20% were designed by Chinese. In the entertainment industry, where Chinese clients were in the majority, they had even better chances. Latest research estimates that 80% of Shanghai's theatres and cinemas were designed by Chinese, including the Paramount Dance Hall by Yang Xiliu, the Majestic Theatre by Fan Wenzhao, and the Shanghai Concert Hall by Fan Wenzhao and Zhao Shen.[16] In 2004, some Chinese, unaware of the origins of these remaining buildings, were sending letters to newspapers asking why the work of foreign colonialists was being preserved. In comparison to the international architecture now flooding the market these early Chinese architects could be judged as having been more truly pioneering than their present day colleagues.

A parallel westernisation, called 'xihua' or 'yanghua', took place in painting and Lu Xun[17] founded a political 'agit-prop' school of Chinese woodcut influenced by German Expressionism. The Storm Society of artists, which took its name from the Berlin Expressionist art publication *Der Sturm* and the Sturm gallery, existed briefly from 1931–35 and was dedicated to the Fauve, Cubist, Dadaist and Surrealist movements.[18] Four exhibitions featured works by their most important members, Pang Xunqin, Ni Yide, Yang Taiyang and Qiu Ti, who had studied in France and Germany. In exchange contemporary Chinese art also toured Europe on the initiative of China's first Minister of Education, Cai Yuanpei, who had himself studied in Leipzig.

These artists' works were derivative, in no way Chinese. Only the models for the figurative paintings gave any indication as to their Asian origin. Their creators wanted to be measured by international standards which were being set by the West. Modern was already synonymous with European-based culture. Not surprisingly this produced an identity crisis for those trying to live in two irreconcilable cultures, and opposition from those who could not enjoy the western style benefits for which they were paying with their labour. Some returned Chinese were at home in neither culture and found themselves fighting on both fronts. When Germany's National Socialists took power in 1933 Lu Xun, with the Chinese League for Human Rights, demonstrated at the Shanghai German Consulate against curbs on intellectual freedom.[19] Simultaneously they were working on behalf of Chinese working in sweatshops and firetrap factories, or starving on the streets.

In opposition to these left-wing internationalists a counter movement of conservative nationalists, demanding a return to traditional Chinese values in music, dress, food and architecture,

Pudong's crowns and spires

John Portman's Bund Finance Centre, 2002, and two P&T buildings, 1934, Huangpu District

was already to be heard in the 1920s.[20] *Chinese Architecture* magazine wrote, "Chinese architects should mix eastern and western knowledge to enhance the characteristics of traditional Chinese architectures."[21] But what was Chinese architecture and could it be adapted for modern functions?

## ANOTHER WAY

"The Chinese people, one quarter of humanity, have stood up … From now on no one will insult us again." Mao Zedong's 1949 declaration, at the birth of the People's Republic,[22] was also a national architectural agenda. No more collaboration with Western colonialism. The feudal past was to be swept away, creating a *tabula rasa* on which to rebuild, physically and metaphorically. Architectural and building-technical expertise was provided by a politically more sympathetic but, yet again, foreign role model, the Soviet Union. China's friendship treaty with the Soviets was to last only eleven years but even after their construction experts left Soviet concepts of bureaucratic respectability and 'palaces for the people' persisted in the work of their Chinese students. Matching up to international standards remained the aim, but within a different ideological system, and Mao's Great Leap Forward motto of 1958 was, 'More, Faster, Better and More Economical'.

Architecture is not least of all an expression of political will, and even more so for a post-colonial or post-feudal society trying to create a binding national image. Post-1949 constructions in Soviet style rose above Beijing's Forbidden City to symbolize

the ascendancy of 'the people'. The east-west Chang-an Jie, 'street of enduring peace', developed as a counterweight to the Imperial north-south axis which had previously influenced all Beijing planning. Both axes cross over Tiananmen Square, dimensioned for an assembly of half a million. At the age of ninety-two, Zhang Kaiji, the architect of the 1959 National Museum of Revolutionary History on Tiananmen Square, reflected: "We wanted to show how great our country was. At the time there was a feeling than bigger was better, but I think that is wrong. It is just to show off. It wasn't really to serve the people. Tiananmen Square is too big."[23]

Tiananmen Square is an oblong paved field of breath-taking proportions surrounded by several eras of monumental state architecture with a north-south orientation, still on the original Imperial axis. To stand in the Square is to understand physically the immensity of the land. Around its perimeter the steeply rising and sloping ramparts of the Forbidden City and the last remaining Qianmen gatehouse, are matched by the 1950s, Soviet-inspired, state architecture, broad, stepped podiums, exaggerated heights of columns, endless loggias and giant dimensioned windows. However, what appears to be a mixed-up Greek architectural vocabulary, filtered through the Romans and borrowed from another European source, reveals classical Chinese features. The 'column-and-tie-beam' technique was used on the National History Museum. The 'unity of structure and architectural art' technique can be seen in the distinctively Chinese carvings under the eaves.[24] Both Greco-Roman and Chinese classical architecture used podiums, or ground floor plinths, and symmetry. Mao's Memorial Hall has a podium on a podium to prolong the antici-pation of entering an almost holy interior. Chinese grouped their buildings according to status and devised a module of courtyards, sometimes with a freestanding pagoda or pavilion at the centre, in the same way that Mao's Memorial Hall sits in Tiananmen Square. Even Tiananmen's lamp posts show a collision of Art Nouveau brass arabesques, supporting white glass lamp orbs, with Chinese paper-cut patterns on the speaker boxes and more recent South-East Asian video cameras. The exchange between East and West, prevalent in Regency Britain and very evident in the nineteenth century, when Chinoiserie was part of European arts and crafts, has gradually become a one way road.

The governmental People's Palace on the west, Mao's Memorial Hall to the south, and China's History Museum and Revolutionary History Museum in a twin structure on the east, have façades which seem to have been run off by the kilometre. They reduce the numerous soldiers, standing guard and marching

'Better City, Better Life', Shanghai's Expo 2010 motto

between their duties, to the scale of toy figures. The poses of revolutionary architecture seem little different from that of the Imperial versions. Qianmen gate house, a remnant of the Imperial city walls, has impenetrably thick walls rising several storeys before allowing any openings. High above street level a plateau of a terrace is ringed by a cantilevered balcony, and the window openings create a regular rhythm up to the roof. All China's dynasties have turned to fortified, untouchable images to maintain distance from the millions and legitimate their power, against or 'for the people'.

Distinct from the renewal program for public representative architecture, or health and education buildings, most of the historical housing in the capital and provinces continued to be used as it was. To relieve the chronic shortage, several families were assigned to villas, flats, or former one-clan *hutongs* previously occupied by just one family. In Shanghai's French Concession, which is rapidly becoming a meticulously renovated area for wealthier families and company offices, many of the villas are still occupied by an elderly generation who moved there in the fifties. Salons, libraries and dining rooms have been subdivided, plaster ceiling roses and cornices have fallen away, stair newels and massive front doors are chipped and scarred. A sad air of disrepair and neglect hangs over what could be revitalized for the existing residents. The architect Chang Yung Ho describes his childhood impression of Beijing in the sixties as "... a Horizontal City ... one saw nothing but a grey ocean of tiled roofs ... interrupted by the green of the trees floating over the courtyards and the golden yellow from the City within the City ..."[25] There was no profit to be gained from density and in the countryside political changes made very little difference to housing standards right up until the twenty-first century. "Houses are built of wattle covered with dried mud or stone, fired brick or concrete blocks according to the prosperity of the locality and individual family. Two or three generations normally live under one roof. The commonest form of floor is pressed earth, though the better-off may have concrete. Village streets are narrow, mostly unpaved, with open drains. Lighting in each home is by a bare light bulb except in more remote villages not yet hooked up to the electrical system where light for the hour or two spent out of bed after dark comes from paraffin lamps, natural pitch, or whatever other kind of oil of fat is available locally."[26] Employees in state industries and institutions across the country were more privileged. Zhejiang University flats, originally built for teaching staff, are parallel rows of four to five-storey blocks standing at right angles to the main road. Entry to each long courtyard between the rows is

through a gate in a two-metre-high wall. The bare concrete stairs, with their metal balustrades, lead to two flats on every landing. Front doors, often left unlocked, open directly into a combined family living and bedroom. Once, families with one or two children shared this twelve-square-metre space. A full-width balcony faces the planted courtyard. Between the main room and the kitchen is a mosaic tiled wet cell with a drain outlet in the floor, an Asian toilet and a tap for a shower pipe. The cooking is done on a tiled concrete worktop on gas rings supplied from a gas cylinder. The generous number of public toilets in Chinese cities, with cleaning attendants who charge admittance, stems from when human waste was collected for agricul-

Qianmen gate, redesigned in 1914, by the German architect Curt Rothkegel

tural fertilizer and when licenses to run a public convenience were much coveted. Factory buildings adopted a Bauhaus style, with flat roofs, concrete frames, plastered blockwork, with runs of small paned metal framed windows but, without the Bauhaus ideal of an industrialized building industry to supply precast and standardized components, the first ones were built using intensive manual labour, from the hauling of materials in wicker baskets and one-off ironmongery fixtures, to the hand mixing of concrete in situ. At least the architecture looked like international functionalism, and had the advantage of being economical.

### CONTROLLING THE UNCONTROLLABLE

Long before the fall of Europe's Iron Curtain, Deng Xiaoping and the post-Mao leadership of China's Communist Party had

A showcase of globally patented cladding systems, Shanghai

formulated an Open Door policy in 1978 to help solve the problem of feeding and employing a population exploding at the annual rate of the USA, USSR and Europe combined.[27] The economic metamorphosis had, in reality, begun long before. Leaders had been turning a blind eye to free market practices for years and state companies which had been loosing money were being privatized so that they at least brought in taxes. The Open Door policy only tried to regulate and speed up the pace of change. Foreign entrepreneurs, in contrast to former colonialists, were now to be welcomed so long as they offered investment capital and technology transfer—and played according to China's rules. Designated areas of the economy; industry, agriculture, science, and national defence were targeted in a list called 'The 4 Modernisms'. To help with the necessary international dialogue the Chinese were urged to practice 'The 5 Cs—Culture, Compromise, Contradiction, Context, and Contribution'. Urban growth was the inevitable spin-off. China was to be inundated by alien lifestyles, shopping fever, youth culture, McDonalds and Starbucks on every corner, international hotels, new environments and more foreigners.

In the early 1980s visas became available for the first time for independent tourists to travel on the Chinese mainland. Hangzhou had an airport that was still semi military and consisted of a couple of huts. No one spoke English and there was no currency exchange on arrival. One of the few hotels was the Hangzhou Hotel, the former foreigner's guesthouse, quickly snapped up by Shangri-La International Hotels. Taxi drivers refused to accept tips. Street signs and bus destinations had not yet been converted to show both characters and 'Pinyin', which uses the Roman alphabet, so remained indecipherable to the average tourist. Beside the West Lake, Xi Hu, Cultural Revolution slogans were still to be seen on the Jingci temple walls while, inside, a huge Buddha sat in unadorned splendour. However, the lake with its causeway and islands, created by nature in the fourth century A.D. and later embellished by numerous emperors, was still as beautiful as Marco Polo had described it.[28] Chinese, in uniform blue or green cotton, smiled, stared at, or even plucked at the clothes of the rare number of solitary foreigners. There were no advertising billboards or high buildings.

At the same time in Guangzhou the history museum, housed in a pagoda, was being overhauled and foreigners were steered away from the section dealing with the opium wars, to avoid embarrassing them with the facts of colonialism. Having been treated with the utmost courtesy in China, tourists who returned to Hong Kong and dared to say they had liked any-

thing north of the border, were treated with scorn by most western building professionals working in what was still a British colony. "But it's so backward," commented an Australian engineer who had worked in Beijing on a government project with an international consultancy. "When we bring back computers to Hong Kong for repairs the Chinese think we are stealing them, and their own engineers mirror our work to check and control our results."[29] Twenty years later the sons and daughters of these same expatriates are working all over China and even trying to learn one of the nation's eight languages. By the early 1990s foreign architects were involved in 30% of Shanghai's development and were moving on to Beijing. By 2004 over

**P&T's Suzhou Sheraton Hotel, 1998**

140 of the world's top 200 design consortiums had offices on the mainland.[30]

On 15 October 2003, China's first space navigator, 'Yuhangyuan', orbited the world. On landing Lieutenant-Colonel Yang Liwei was greeted like a pop star by a chorus of girls wearing traditional red-silk dresses and a military guard of honour. China was now in third place among the space travelling nations, after the USSR and USA. It was a symbolic moment for many Chinese and marked a complete turn around in the world's perception of their country. A growing national self-confidence was apparent in China's eagerness to join international organizations, such as the World Trade Organization (WTO) in 2001, and host the 2008 Olympics, 2010 Expo, or Architecture and Art Biennales in Beijing and Shanghai in 2004, all of which further advertised Chinese

**Century Boulevard, Pudong**

achievements. All these activities needed a new national image to convince the population—and demonstrate to foreigners—China's break with past insularity and suspicion. Where was this internationally understandable, publicity image to come from if not, as in the past, from western architecture? "Students know more about America and the English language than Chinese," lamented a Professor of Architecture.[31] The American, Chinese born, architect I. M. Pei's explanation is that, "[New] Chinese architecture is not trying to convey a meaning or style. Their skyscrapers are like ours because they are adapting to the Western way of business. Like my wearing a Western suit, it's appropriate."[32]

By 2004 there were over 174 cities with more than one million inhabitants. Chongqing, at the centre of the Three Gorges Dam development, is the world's most populated urban conglomeration with over thirty-one million inhabitants.[33] From Harbin to Shenzhen old cities exploded in size, spawning satellite towns, and new cities were planned in the Pearl River delta. They were all in love with the idea of towers and wide highways as icons of prestige. By critical standards not all projects are 'appropriate' but they attract investment and snowball growth and in the rush for the 'new' ancient street plans and even whole communities have been swept away.[34]

Beijing, as the seat of centralized government and bureaucracy remained fixed in its environmental expression right up until 1978 developments began to mow down vast tracts of the historical centre. Officially *hutongs* still housed 50% of the population[35] but between 1985 and 2003 over 1,665 had been destroyed.[36] In the most extreme cases, people who lost their homes in corruption scandals in 2003, set fire to themselves in public protests. In contrast, the Beijing journalist and engineer couple, who bought a high-rise flat with all-mod-cons, were examples of the growing urban 'sandwich class'[37] well educated, childless and with two incomes. They had been living with the husband's seventy-two-year-old father, where their only private space had been their seven square metre bedroom, and were able to buy a 101-square-metre unit in a new development of ten storeys set around public gardens. Apartments are handed over in a raw state and, after fitting out, the cost was 900,000 Yuan (approx. $110,00 or £60,000). Their deposit came from the family and the mortgage from the developer. Monthly repayments were 40% of their gross income, and subject to future interest rates.[38]

Where were all the building professionals to come from for these projects? In the first year that China's universities

Mass housing in Hangzhou with rooftop kindergarten, late 1970s

opened again after the Cultural Revolution there were places for only 200,000 students, out of forty million applicants. Later state scholarships to the West, for which students had to be fluent in English or other European languages, helped prepare for international networking. The China Academy of Art, based in Hangzhou, is just one of the many architecture schools now available at home.[39] The building process in China is a compartmentalized system in which design, detailing and on-site experience, are often carried out by different offices. Few initiating architects have control over the end product. China's professional practice license system, given to individuals or institutions, has lead to the emergence of three types of office; Chinese institutions developed out of university and state departments, foreign architects' offices increasingly run by Chinese, and a growing number of younger offices modelling themselves on international studios.[40]

A few Chinese architects, born in the sixties, are beginning to be publicized in the West and there is a continuous exchange of young architects between western and Chinese offices. Feichang Jianzhu Studio in Beijing is one such office. The partners Chang Yung Ho, Lu Lijia and Wang Hui, took part in the 2000 Venice Biennale and have exhibited in New York. Chang, the eldest of the three, studied and worked in the USA and is now Dean of the Beijing University Graduate Centre of Architecture. Their International Conference Centre in Qingdao, for a branch of Beijing University, has a coastal site with a twenty metre fall to the beach. Horizontal layers of building elements in precast concrete, with glass balustrades and aluminium panels, jut out

**RTKL's Science and Technology Museum, Shanghai-Pudong, 2004**

Punting on Xi Hu, Hangzhou's West Lake

MADA were preparing to move to a larger office in a former government kindergarten which they were renovating themselves. Their Cultural Centre for Ningbo shows the influence of Alvar Aalto in the asymmetrical and articulated assembly of a drum caught in the pincers of oblong blocks in a triangular plan. The architects themselves own up to using a 'Japanese touch' in the black granite facings. Their temporary estate agent's sales office in Beijing, with its model exhibition area, video animation and confidential meeting cubicles separated by translucent screens, was a Miesian pavilion with a fully-glazed box slid under an independent flat roof slab which was supported on freestanding columns away from the façade. Operating on their home ground brings MADA work for which foreigners would not be commissioned but, because they are small, clients usually give detailing to an institution. 'Those architectural factories don't think, they just do, because they are paid for quantity, not quality."[41]

Land is still state-owned. Private investors buy seventy year leases, or government clients carry through public projects which are always the subject of international competitions. Several prize winners are announced and they are all exhibited to give the public a chance to vote and comment. Having covered themselves against charges of corruption the client and a professional jury then make their own decision. The original architect may no longer be included in the process when an institution takes over the rest of the program. Winning a competition, carrying out the first stage design and being paid, is no guarantee that the project will ever be built. Christoph Ingenhoven designed Shanghai's Shimao International Plaza, which opens in 2006, but has not been involved since the planning stage. Long after AS&P had been paid for a Beijing project their partner found himself, by chance, standing in the middle of a building site where their design was finally being constructed by another team.[42] Even Olympic projects have been ruthlessly amended and redesigned, during construction, in response to public protest about budgets that bear no relation to the nation's wealth.

from the hillside to form a roof terrace overlooking the sea. This is location related contemporary architecture without lingering 'Chinese kitsch'. The Nanjing practice Nanda Jianzhu were more influenced by Aldo Rossi and Swiss purity when they built student dormitories for Nantong Foreign Language School in plain red brick, without decoration, in marshalled identical wings joined by a surrounding brick wall. When Herzog & de Meuron began designing their entry for the Beijing Olympic's National Stadium they were introduced to Ai Weiwei, an artist and architect, through the former Swiss ambassador to China. Apart from advising on ethnic identity Ai Weiwei has also designed speculative architecture with Chang Yung Ho. Their 'Courtyards by the Canal', a high-income housing enclave, is advertised in a brochure with whimsical drawings, without third dimension perspective, in the classical, Chinese painting style. Ai's art has attracted western collectors who are certainly easier customers than global businesses who, until now, have never employed a Chinese architect without international status.

MADA s.p.a.m. is a Shanghai practice. One of the partners, Qing Yun Ma, born in 1965, was part of Rem Koolhaas' Harvard urbanism research team before setting up MADA in Beijing in 2000. He moved to Shanghai because the work climate was more open. About forty young international architects work on rows of computers in a multi-storey bank tower on Nanjing Lu, the main shopping mile. Office space is at a premium, few sit near a window, or even have a view out of the open plan and cramped room where models and paper debris spill onto the floor. A partner's office is not much bigger than a cupboard. By 2004

Architects employed by speculators are under pressure from the beginning to increase density for maximum return over finite lease periods, something that rapidly transforms the low lying historical 'Horizontal City' into a 'Vertical City'. The result is a 'City of Objects', designed according to building codes which try to compromise with the market economy, using rules for Daylight Distance, Floor Area Ratio (FAR), Building Coverage, Greenery Coverage, and Setback.[43] The 'Horizontal City' is meshed into the surroundings; the 'Vertical City' has no context, with each object standing alone.

Neo-classical and Louis XIV styled apartments on the way to Pudong International Airport

Not many Chinese clients recognized the publicity and profit advantages of innovative architecture but, "There are a few significantly influential developers, of which SOHO is one."[44] SOHO is Zhang Xin, who was born in Beijing but worked in Hong Kong investment banks before becoming a developer. She says she is "revitalizing Beijing's street culture."[45] Pan Shiyi, her husband, says: "We are taking into account the characteristics and fashions of our era. We consider our primary mission to be the production of cutting edge architecture."[46] Exclusive fashion sells architecture just as well as haute couture labels sell clothes. SOHO built 'The Commune', twelve modern villas beside the Great Wall, which won a 2002 Venice Biennale award, commercial projects in Beijing, and the Bao Canal Village on Hainan Island. Working with Chinese and foreign architects, Rocco Yim, C.Y. Lee, Zaha Hadid and MVRDV, SOHO's development strategy distances itself from historical pastiche.

The pragmatic view is to buy Western 'trophy' architecture as a profitable attraction. Following the success of Frank Gehry's Bilbao Guggenheim Museum, he was invited to design a museum for Nanjing. "I got all excited about it. We met the guys a few

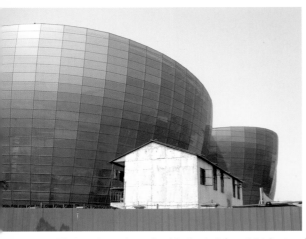

**Workers barracks on Paul Andreu's Oriental Art Centre site, 2004**

times and then, one day, they let me know that it had to be profitable as a real estate venture. Those guys were out to lunch! Of course, when we told them it couldn't be done, they abandoned the project. Chinese architecture seems so skin deep."[47] In 2004 the Toronto firm, Six Degrees Architecture and Design Inc., were planning a 'Canadian Maple Town' in Fengjing New Town, one

of nine new satellite towns outside the 800-year-old Fengjing canal town, beside the Yangtze river. 'When our client says, just make it Canadian, what does that mean?" asked the architect. She was told it should symbolize Canada in the space of four square kilometres for 28,000 residents with a city hall, art gallery, museum, convention centre and five star hotel to be completed by 2010. The culture centre, sitting on a Canadian Cedar deck, has a steel ribbon wrapped around it like a giant present, and there will be a maple leaf on the roof. Canadian and Fengjing art installations will line the roads. Homes on the water-front will be constructed in Canadian timber and limestone.[48] Planned instant cities, following in the steps of Le Corbusier's theoretical Contemporary City and built Chandigah, Lúcio Costa's winning plan for Brasilia which was based on the sign of the Cross, or more banal examples of patriarchal social democracy like Runcorn New Town, Basildon or Milton Keynes in Britain, have long been discredited in the West. Will their location in China make them any more successful? The trend for facsimile European atmospheres in Shanghai's eleven satellite towns has included German, Spanish and Italian examples. GMP's Luchao Harbour City is centred on a man made lake, like Hamburg in Germany, but on a larger scale, more exacting in its building use zones and more ruthlessly streamlined than the original. The seduction of creating whole cities based on a simple idea remains as addictive as it did at the beginning of the modern movement. Even international architects with reputations to lose take part in this game.

Regardless of the product Chinese private and public clients still retain a degree of suspicion, understandable in the wake of their colonial history, and want to ensure that they, as paymasters, are in complete control and getting value for money or, even better, a first class service at bargain prices. Some show a degree of schizophrenia in wanting to flaunt their increasing power and sophistication while simultaneously resenting the fact that the style of their new image is not their own. According to Rem Koolhaas: "The Chinese love the monumental ambition. They hate the monumental price tag—and 'foreign' design."[49]

The authoritarian state has not withered away. It is a necessary framework for construction. Foreign and Chinese architects often express their gratitude to the government for providing a guarantee for the process of building. "They decided to go for the free market but without the Chinese Communist Party the system would be chaos."[50] The authoritarian state can always summon up reinforcements at a moments notice. When P&T architects were rushing to complete the Beijing Oriental

**From 'greenfield' residential and industrial suburbs in the hinterland ...**

Plaza, a mixed complex with a five-star 600-room Hyatt Hotel on Chang-an Jie, in time for the fiftieth anniversary of the People's Republic of China celebrations, the government commandeered thousands of soldiers to finish the site works.[51] As in colonial times what would never be accepted at home is tolerated abroad in the name of expediency.

On a commuter plane from Beijing to Shanghai an impeccably dressed Chinese television executive explained to me the principles of China's new economy. He had just told me that our European social system was an unaffordable luxury and we were all overpaid anyway because, even on his modest Chinese state scholarship to a Belgian university, he had been able to study, travel and even send money home to his family. "Imagine the Chinese economy as a bicycle. The harder and faster we peddle the more stable the ride." To stop pedalling is to fall off. The hope is that in allowing free market activity, but under authoritarian control, riches will filter down to the agrarian and urban poor, but unprecedented construction activity has lead to material shortages and rising costs,[52] destroyed historical architecture, produced horrendous traffic problems, health threatening air pollution,[53] power[54] and water supply problems.[55] Every day in the capital 1,000 new cars take to the roads[56] while less than 30% of Beijing's inhabitants use public transport, partly because the efficient and clean Underground is expensive for residents and other transport networks are still in development, but also because a car is the ultimate status symbol in an economy where poverty has virtually become a sin. The very fact that bicycles are cheap reduces their desirability for those who can afford more. China is not alone in failing to find a balance between public and private transport. It is only a measure of its development that it now joins the list of other polluting first world countries.

The cheap labour of forty million itinerant building workers, 'Min Gong', has made the new architecture possible—but the only time they live in it is during construction. Many sleep on site to support families at home and save up for their own businesses. Their connection to the city is functional and tenuous. "No regrets taking down old houses," a worker called Wu in Shanghai said. "No purpose in knowing history. People have to follow the times."[57] They have no influence over developments so they might as well profit from the changes, but their nomadic existence alienates them from their families, casual relationships add to the AIDS problem and, without employment contracts or social security insurance, they are at risk from dangerous construction practices. Building workers' clapboard dormitories in wood and plasterboard huts with bunk beds and an outside standpipe for

water, seen against a technologically tooled and sophisticated building like Paul Andreu's cluster of cut-glass bowl auditoriums at Shanghai's Oriental Arts Centre, highlight the stark and growing social divergence.

The main 2008 Olympic Games site is on Beijing's Northern outskirts beyond the 5th Ring Road. At present the setting is a chequer-board environment of busy intersections, crumbling concrete flyovers and rusty pedestrian bridges. Half constructed commercial skyscrapers, their steel frames not yet clad, new, white, sparkling, owner-occupier apartments protected behind walls and rotting older residential units reduced to slums, line the route to the Games. On the arrow straight Deshengmenwai road heavy goods wagons, alongside Japanese and German cars made in China, roll bumper to bumper along an asphalt conveyor belt. People are moving faster on the crowded pavements. Trees,

**Wusong building site, 2004**

on both sides of the road and in the central reservation, are limp with the weight of grime. Along the broken pavements, not yet beautified for the televised event, restaurants, easily recognized by their red paper lanterns and hand painted pictures of glazed Beijing duck dishes, jostle with Indian curry houses, Mongolian hot-pot or Japanese noodle shops, interspersed with supermarkets,

**... past pantiled villages and family villas to the big city high-rise apartments**

jeans and sportswear shops, opticians and herbal or western medicine stores. Apartment and office windows advertise business website addresses, plumbing and medical services. Air-conditioners lean precariously out of makeshift holes cut in the walls or stand on balconies, beside cupboards, bicycles and lines of washing. These are the anonymous transit areas, without historical monuments or planning input, where most of the city's inhabitants live and work. Will it all be swept away and tidied up or left to co-exist beside the streamlined and efficient architecture for the Games?

"The Olympic facilities will become the defining architecture of the new century in Beijing."[58] The stadiums have all taken on carnival costumes to either boldly declare, or hide, their functions. Herzog & de Meuron's National Stadium is planning to look like a bird's nest of twigs and the National Swimming Centre, or 'Water Cube', is container architecture covered in 'Teflon' ETFE quilting, to simulate water, and the whole façade is no less than a huge electronic media screen for projected light shows. The Velodome's architectural silhouette is that of a cyclist's helmet and the Shooting Range is moulded into a bow and arrow plan. As in calligraphy these are holistic images. In both Chinese classical literature and daily speech words paint pictures. Narrative is more popular than abstraction. 'Big Character' and 'Small Character' political posters, which reached their height in the Cultural Revolution, have already been absorbed into architecture as pixel screen façades and gargantuan advertising elevations.[59] Ultimately these buildings have become construction frames on which to hang national aspirations and sponsors' trademarks. The hidden technology behind these nursery images includes the latest in construction efficiency and energy saving. For example, sectional 'strips' of the 'Water Cube', slices of walls and roof, are to be assembled at one end of the site and then shunted and successively bolted together for construction speed and to avoid having to use internal scaffolding. Other pioneering systems for China include solar power for heating water and underground storage tanks for the recycling of rainfall.[60] With picture walls and hi-tech, architecture will host world games and become the medium for the message: China is on the ball.

## TO BE, OR NOT TO BE, CHINESE

"What does it mean being a Chinese in the making of architecture? Will Chinese-ness come about by the architect being Chinese, or by the context of being Chinese, or both, or neither?"[61] China's architecture is still a projected future not yet complete.

Most of what has been built shows no evidence of having been designed by architects. Much that has been demolished should have been modernized and conserved. So far, China's multi-million cities offer fragments of a one world monoculture, clothed in architecture first developed at the Bauhaus, refined in the skyscrapers and shopping malls of the New World, and project managed with quasi-military efficiency. Even if the skylines of central Beijing, Shanghai, Chongqing, Hangzhou, Shenzhen or Guangzhou, have so far nothing in common with the sparsely developed hinterlands, or even other districts in the same cities, they are like a first deposit payment for a brighter future. Are the remnants of a once common social structure and a shared history of upheaval enough to bind together peasants living a hand-to-mouth existence with the new class of property owners and rich continental travellers? Is the twenty-first century promise of disposable incomes and Internet connections, as a thin veneer to cover widening economic and ethnic differences, strong enough to withstand a major crisis?

The wish for a new national and recognizably Chinese identity is growing. Meanwhile, traditional features, like badges, have been stuck on to hi-tech architecture to make it more culturally palatable. In a contradiction of the Euro-Modernist theory of 'form follows function' the classical idea of an honourable 'face' has been applied to contemporary buildings. Previously, all over China, an historical building rule laid down that the south façade, turned towards the sun for warmth and light, should be the public face of any complex, independent of functions hidden behind its walls. Unlike European modern architecture, which propagates design from the inside to the outside and results in the internal activities and uses influencing the envelope, many Chinese still prefer to remain private and hidden behind a mask. For the insecure new elites the idea of a frontage, designed to legitimise their status, is an attractive architectural option. Likewise old city walls no longer fend off competing warlords but segregate different price ranges of housing and, even in the first stages of construction, tower block sites are enclosed by brick walls with pantile copings to underline their exclusivity. Modern corporate management structures also find a functional use for the physical form of social hierarchy, the feudal mono-axis, which traditionally progressed through a city or house from South to North and branched out into lesser courtyards and buildings.[62]

An alternative youth movement, 'linglei', expressing individuality in dress, entertainment and communication technology, is a recent phenomenon in East coast cities. All previous

**Beijing's existing Asian Games stadium**

Hangzhou's China Academy of Art

Chinese eras, regardless of the political system, prized duty, respect for authority, and discipline, in the name of social cohesion.[63] Even today a Chinese businessman in Pudong, reprimanded by a traffic policewoman for trying to jaywalk, virtually hung his head in shame before obediently retreating to the pavement. Crowd control is paramount throughout China. In Beijing sections of metre-high looped ironwork, reminiscent of English Victorian park fences surrounding lawns and floor beds to ward off trespassers, are used to cordon off pavements, roads and districts, in contradiction of 'free flow' principles.

When Remo Riva was asked in the late nineties to design a Sheraton Hotel in Suzhou he intended healing the area, by extending the city wall around the site and using the old quarry to provide granite cladding for the new building. In the tourist season visitors double the city's 2.2 million resident population, attracted by what looks like an animated Wedgwood 'Willow Pattern' china tea service of classically landscaped gardens, 2,500 year old canals, tree lined cobbled lanes, picturesque narrow stone bridges, low-level, pantiled and white-plastered terraces. The hotel architecture recreated the idea of an Imperial Palace, visually connecting it with adjacent remnants of Suzhou's 1,800 year old city walls and the Puiguang Ta Pagoda, dating from 247 A.D. A steeply ramped vehicle access and inward sloping walls put on a defensive front to the main road. Not until first floor level does the plan open out in the lobby. Restaurants and executive suites sit in square pavilions with dragon eaves, on top of the ramparts. Behind the walls guest rooms are grouped in white plastered 'village' houses with wooden balconies, among goldfish ponds with stone bridges, rockeries and bamboo stands. The well-intentioned aim, to blend in with an historical city structure, has produced an autark bastion of luxury protected from the city, like a patriarchal emperor looking back into the future. Meanwhile Suzhou's government is planning an 'eco-model city', decreeing that bludgeoning industries and a thriving international trade centre comply with sustainable services, and experimenting with taxis run on natural gas.

The Beijing Hotel on Chang-an Jie was once the capital's guesthouse for V.I.P. foreign dignitaries. It is now a five-star international hotel. Its many extensions over fifty years include a foyer modelled on the interior of the throne room in Tiahe Palace. Where the steps in the palace lead up to a podium on which the Imperial eminence sat to hold court, the steps here lead up to double full-height doors opening into a grand public dining or ballroom beyond. Embossed and gilded corbelled columns support ceiling coffer beams. Every available surface is textured, carved, and painted with red highlights. Colour was a strong architectural feature from the Song dynasty onwards, used in a strict code of red for walls, pillars, doors and window frames, yellow for roofs, and blue or green for under the eaves. 'Jian', the bays between corbelled brackets, the 'cai' Song dynasty module with eight size variations, or the 'doukou' Qing dynasty module, with eleven variations, were all early forms of construction standardization, hierarchy carried into the last architectural detail.

Hangzhou's West Lake, or Suzhou's ancient gardens, created by feudal rulers solely for their solitary intellectual pleasure, for boating, composing poetry and music, painting and contemplation, are now China's 'chill out rooms' for the masses. To float in a flat bottomed boat on the West Lake, to aimlessly wander over stepping stones, listen to bird song or traditional music played in a tea pavilion in Suzhou's Garden of the Humble Administrator is an instant antidote to the environment beyond the garden walls. The beauty of such manmade, totally artificial and useless architectural styles lies in its superfluousness. Modern equivalents are Shanghai's Renmin Park, re-modelled with hillocks, pools and seating, the popular backdrop of official wedding photographs, or Hangzhou's lakeside park incorporating the rebuilt Leifeng pagoda. On the edge of the park a series of interconnected timber and glass pavilions for restaurants and small offices drawn up by the architects Z. Zhang and Ming Zhang of Original Design Studio, take their inspiration from classical palace follies, where the scent of flowering bushes and the sound of lapping water played a soothing concert with the lake's mirrored surface, reflecting and melting into a changing

Commercial and business properties on the way to Beijing's Olympic 2008 site

sky. Nowadays, Hangzhou's crude silhouette of jagged towers, standing threateningly over this idyllic waterscape, mark a decisive break in a society which is going through a process of differentiation in more ways than one; economically, socially and, last but not least, aesthetically.

"How to get the old and the new together? I think this is a problem of systems, not aesthetics," says Professor Shiling, who advises Shanghai government planners and sits on juries for architecture competitions. "In China everything happens simultaneously, it's dialectics, and we have to create our own modern."

In an attempt to try and do just that, Li Chengde, an artist and not an architect, designed the modern China Academy of Art. He has produced a hybrid architecture of classical south-east Asian and modern features in a local narrow grey-blue brick, with black metal framed window units, in strong horizontal and vertical gestures. A bulbous auditorium breaks through this self-imposed straight jacket. Overhangs to shadow openings and triangular window boxes extending out of the walls seem to be influenced by Frank Lloyd Wright who was already collecting Japanese woodblock art by the end of the nineteenth century. Classical Chinese corbelled column and beam connections rise to Expressionist, horizontally grilled, lanterns on feudal gate towers and columns, four storeys high, march up the entrance steps to an Imperial plinth and ceremonial way leading into an internal street foyer. Since its foundation in 1928 the aim of the Academy has been to unite eastern and western arts. It does not need the Porsche car showroom, which shares the complex, to show that this architecture reveals inherent contradictions. Should traditional cultural symbols, originating in feudal, aristocratic or colonized societies, sit comfortably with modernity or does this very real discontinuity pinpoint the underlying conflict?

When the American playwright Arthur Miller was directing his play *Death of a Salesman*, for a Beijing premiere, he told his cast of Chinese actors: "This play's performance cannot be a success, and it will possibly be a catastrophe, when you try to mimic another culture."[64] At the time China was still operating in a parallel universe, with a political philosophy in opposition to the West. In today's context, with China turning to western business practices and individualism, Arthur Miller's advice might be wrongly interpreted as an enforcement of chauvinism. China is transforming itself under the label of modernity and western architecture provides the fitting image. When, and if, a Chinese Modernism evolves it will probably not make use of historical elements as we imagine them today.

"There are some young Chinese architects trying to search for a vernacular," says the Chinese-born, American architect I.M. Pei, 'but the wave of foreign imported ideas is powerful. And so China imports talent. It seeks architects of great stature because it wants to learn from us, but even the good architects are not doing their best work in China because they don't feel challenged. It takes two to make good architecture—a savvy client and a creative architect. China needs to develop confidence again in its own culture. Out of confidence will come a new life, new culture, and a unique architecture." Until then China is wearing western camouflage.

## NOTES

1 Luigi Novelli, *Shanghai Architecture*, Shanghai, 2004.

2 The Jin Mao tower conforms to Chinese superstitions about the number eight which is considered lucky. Even building professionals, who had studied abroad, still chose eighty-eight metres for the height of another tower, AS&P's hi-tech administration centre in Zhang Jiang.

3 Heico Forster and Dorothea Sundergeld, *Max* magazine, 2/2004.

4 Tony Saich, *Governance and Politics of China*, London/Oxford, 2004.

5 *Tulou* from *tu* = earth and *lou* = building.

6 See History Appendix.

7 Torsten Warner, *German Architecture in China*, Berlin, 1994.

8 Frances Wood, *No Dogs & Not Many Chinese, Treaty Port Life in China 1843–1943*, London, 1998.

9 *Comprador* = Chinese bi-lingual go-between and general business manager.

10 Charles M. Dyce, *Personal Reminiscences of Thirty Years Residence in the Model Settlement Shanghai 1870–1900*, n.p., 1906.

11 Rediscovered, four-storey, colonial club house with spires, pillars, paintings and sculpture, *Xinhua*, 21/8/03.

12 www.sh-sunyat-sen.com

13 W.H. Auden, Christopher Isherwood, *Journey to a War*, London, 1939.

14 Mao Tun, *Midnight*, Peking, 1957.

15 Jonathan D. Spence and Annping Chin, *The Chinese Century*, New York, 1996.

16 Prof. Zheng Zuan, of the Shanghai Academy of Social Science's Institute of History, *Shanghai Daily News*, 4/7/04.

17 Zhou Shuren, a.k.a. Lu Xun, 1881–1936, pioneer of modern Chinese literature.

18 *Der Sturm*, radical Berlin art magazine and gallery, 1910–32.

19 'Shanghai Modern', joint Shanghai and Munich exhib. and cat., Museum Villa Stuck, Munich, 1/2005.

20 Arranged marriages and wife beating, were also common among western educated Republican party members, see Han Suyin's autobiography, *Birdless Summer*, 1968.

21 Qian Zonghao, a researcher in architectural history at Shanghai History Museum, 2004.

22 Public speech by Mao Zedong, Tianamen Square, Beijing, 1/10/49.

**P&T's Suzhou Sheraton hotel, 1998**

23 BBC World Service interview 3/2004.

24 Banister Fletcher et al., *Sir Banister Fletcher's History of Architecture*, London, 1996.

25 Professor Chang Yung Ho, interview in *A+U* magazine, Tokyo, 12/2003.

26 David Bonavia, *The Chinese: A Portrait*, New York, 1980.

27 Only the one-child policy managed to hold the population down to 1.3 billion in 2003.

28 "... the City of Heaven, the most beautiful and magnificent in the world ..." Marco Polo, late thirteenth century.

29 Christoph Krämer, *China Travel Diary*, unpublished.

30 *Beijing Architecture Journal, China Daily*, 5/7/04.

31 Prof. Zheng Shiling in an interview with the author, Shanghai, 22/10/2004.

32 I.M. Pei, *Fortune* magazine, European Special Edition, 4/10/2004.

33 *China 2004*, Beijing, 2004.

34 Protesting residents who refuse to be evicted, even when services are turned off and their neighbourhood has been demolished around them, are called 'nail residents', because like nails once hammered into the wood they are hard to remove.

35 Beijing Official Web Portal, 6/2004.

36 *The Strait Times*, 4/2003.

37 'Sandwich class', term first coined by Hong Kong media to describe the new Chinese middle-class.

38 BBC World News website documentary, 7/2004.

39 The China Academy of Art: www.eng.caa.edu.cn

40 Prof. Zheng Shiling in an interview with the author, Shanghai, 22/10/04.

41 The architect Ann Mu in an interview with the author, at MADA s.p.a.m., Shanghai, 22/10/04.

42 Johannes Dell, China partner of AS&P in an interview with the author, Frankfurt am Main, 12/03.

43 Prof. Chang Yung Ho, *A+U* magazine, pub. Tokyo, 12/2003.

44 Rocco Yim in an interview with the author, at Rocco Design, Hong Kong, 29/10/04.

45 *Fortune*, 4/10/2004.

46 *A+U*, Tokyo, 12/2003.

47 Frank O. Gehry, *South China Morning Post* newspaper, Hong Kong, 29/11/04.

48 Tony Wong, *Toronto Star* newspaper, 6/2004.

49 Rem Koolhaas, *Wired* magazine, 8/2004.

50 Nikolaus Goetze, GMP partner in an interview with the author, at GMP, Hamburg, 7/2/03.

51 Remo Riva, P&T Group architect director in an interview with the author, at P&T, Hong Kong, 28/10/04.

52 By 2004 China was spending nearly 16% of its gross domestic product (GDP) on construction. Its consumption of 54.7% of the world's concrete production, 36.1% of the world's steel and 30.4% of the world's coal, along with its growing thirst for oil was causing shortages in other developed economies. Report in *Architectural Record*, USA, 6/2004.

53 According to the World Bank 90% of the world's most polluted cities are in China and air pollution, caused mainly by the use of coal, costs China 25 billion US$ a year in health costs and lost labour. BBC World News, 16/6/04.

54 2003 power demand far outweighed supply. New mega complexes, dependent on air conditioning, forced 1,000 firms, including Volkswagen AG and Polaroid, to cut production. Long term emergency measures included asking 700 manufacturers to work evening shifts, forcing public buildings to turn their air conditioning down and forbidding nightclubs to start cooling until after 4 p.m. *Shanghai Daily* reported that turning off floodlights in the city could save 30,000 kilowatt hours a day with the result that the view of Pudong from the Bund is plunged into darkness before midnight.

55 New developments use more water. Five times over the last decade the Yellow River failed to reach the sea and underground reservoirs have lost 90% of their reserves. Loss of ground water has lead to sinking ground levels and instability. *The Observer*, 15/2/2004.

56 Beijing Municipal Traffic Management Bureau (BTMB) recorded that in 1994 Beijing's average traffic speed was forty-five kilometres/hour within the Third Ring Road area. By 2004 it was less than twenty kilometres, in the worst cases less than seven kilometres/hour. BBC World News, 16/6/2004.

57 Juan Du, *Domus* magazine, Milan, 9/2004.

58 *China Daily* newspaper, 12/7/03.

59 Chinese characters, understood by all Chinese regardless of which of the eight languages they speak, are part of a communication system very different from one evolved from a Greco-Roman alphabet and an Age of Enlightenment schooled in abstraction. Every unique character has to be memorized. 2–3,000 characters are needed to read a newspaper. A well-educated Chinese recognizes over 5,000. 9,999 characters are most frequently used and there are a recorded total of 45,000. Simplifications were introduced post-1949 to aid literacy. Official aims are to teach all Chinese the official *Putonghua* Mandarin language, simplify the characters, and install a romanized *Pinyin* Chinese, so far only used to write names in western languages.

60 Thirty-five gymnasiums and stadiums are planned, not only in Beijing, but also Shanghai, Tianjin, Shenyang in the north-eastern province of Liaoning, Qinhuangdao in the northern province of Hebei and Qingdao on the east coast in the province of Shandong. Tianjin, Qinhuangdao, Shenyang and Shanghai are to hold some of the soccer matches. Qingdao will be the centre for sailing. Tianjin began construction of their soccer Olympic stadium (Japanese architects AXS), with a seating capacity of 60,000, in August 2003. The National Swimming Centre for 17,000 spectators (the Australian architects Peddle Thorp and Walker with Ove Arup, the China State Construction Engineering Corporation and the Shenzhen Design Institute) has been financed by overseas Chinese from twenty different countries in a gesture of ethnic solidarity. During 2003, final designs for the Olympic Green (the USA architects Sasaki) and the Wukesong Cultural and Sports Centre (the Swiss architects Burckhardt and Partners) were approved. By the end of 2003 the National Swimming Centre, the National Stadium (the Swiss architects Herzog & de Meuron), and the 8,500-seat Beijing Shooting Range (Architectural Design and Research Institute of Tsinghua University) and the 6,000-seat Laoshan Velodrome (Guangdong Architectural Design and Research Institute) in Shijingshan, West Beijing, were being detailed. These four projects alone will cost over 830 million Yuan. *Xinhua*, 29/7/03.

61 Rocco Yim, *Being Chinese in Architecture*, Hong Kong, 2004.

62 Luigi Novelli, *Shanghai Architectural Guide*, Shanghai, 2003.

63 Sun Longji, *The Deep Structure of Chinese Culture*, Hong Kong, 1983.

64 Arthur Miller, *Salesman in Peking*, New York, 1983.

**Hangzhou's China Academy of Art**

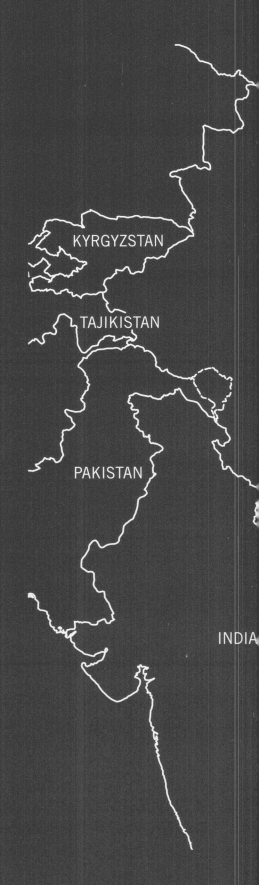

KYRGYZSTAN

TAJIKISTAN

PAKISTAN

INDIA

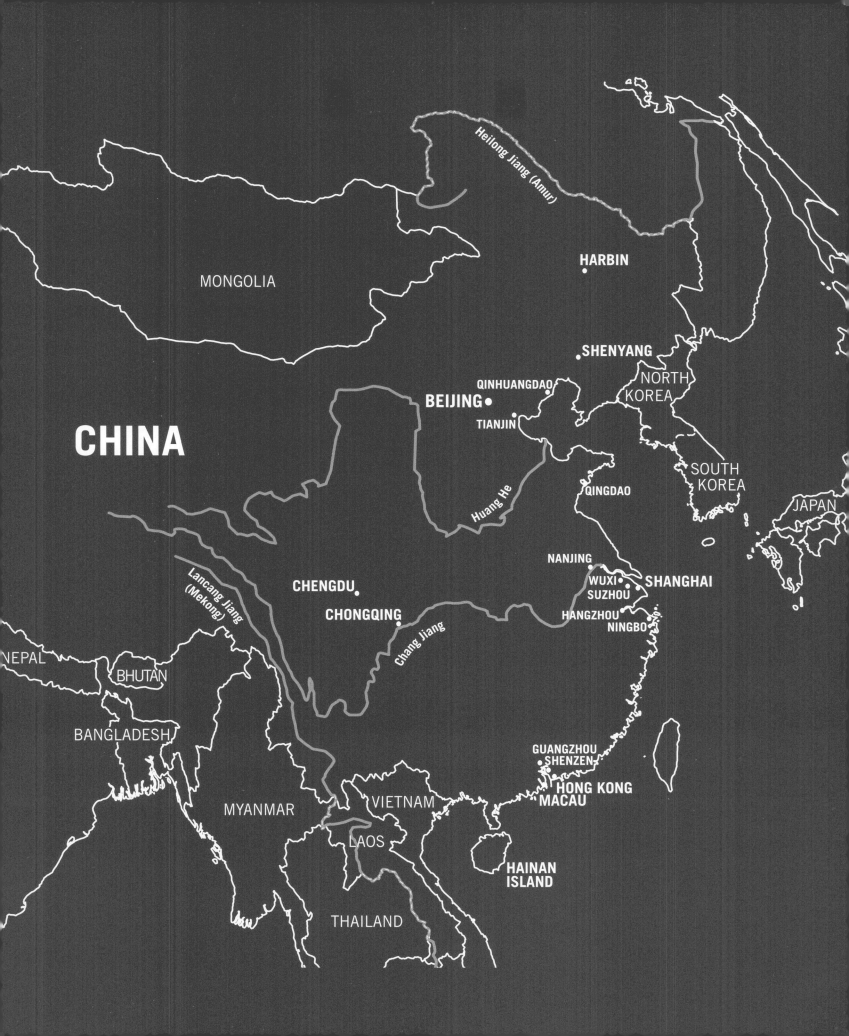

Paul Andreu

# SHANGHAI PUDONG INTERNATIONAL AIRPORT, SHANGHAI

Completed 1999

Pudong Airport is China's main entry for foreign visitors because, although Shanghai is not the capital city, it is the nation's most important white-collar business and financial centre. In 2010 it will also have to handle the arrivals and departures, international and national, for the World EXPO.

The master plan takes account of this with an open ended concept, allowing for later extension, of four modules running north-south, parallel to the runways. A second major aim was to create a 'natural' landscape of lakes and gardens, in and around the complex, as a contribution towards the EXPO theme of technology and environment integration. The first phase is well embedded in manicured lawns and the art of topiary tended by an army of masked and gowned gardeners and sweepers.

Again the architectural imagery is on a one-to-one basis with form illustrating function. Steel filigree roofs extend over the terminals like protective wings which are also interpreted as symbolic of Shanghai's 'take-off' into the twenty-first century. The first phase development is a 210,000-square-metre terminal with two levels, departures above and arrivals below, connected to a 1,400-metre-long embarkation gallery by glazed walkways. The terminal hall is divided transversely into similar international and domestic services. Passenger throughput in the first phase is twenty million, made up of five million international passengers and fifteen million domestic. The final phase will be able to cope with over seventy million passengers annually.

The airport apron has twenty-eight stands for aircraft in close contact with the terminal and eleven remote stands. Internationally departing passengers are processed at eighty check-in desks while domestic flights have 112. High-quality, long-life natural marble and tiling, international standards of comfort with familiar waiting lounge fittings, and a light and spacious atmosphere with occasional glimpses into the gardens, do not adequately prepare first time China visitors for the complete contrast programme outside the terminal doors where they have to run the gauntlet of freelance taxi drivers. There are in fact official, policed, taxi stands and efficient bus services on the canopied forecourt and a 130,000-square-metre car-park building beyond, in front of the terminal. The express highway to Pudong and tunnel under the river to Shanghai, directly link the airport and the city. The journey can take anything from forty-five minutes to three hours depending on traffic.

△ **A sweeping approach and departure on two levels of elevated highways**

▽ **A transparent structure of overlapping wings**

△ Raked and fully glazed walls look out over landscaped gardens

▽ Section through passenger halls and airport apron

▷ Palm trees and enduring quality surfaces bathed in light

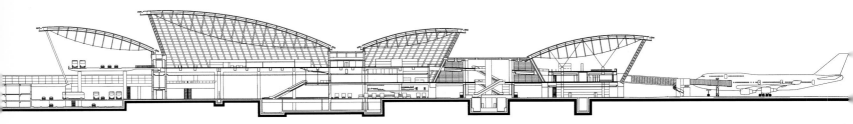

# BEIJING CAPITAL INTERNATIONAL AIRPORT TERMINAL 3, BEIJING

Completion 2008

Beijing Airport was expanded in 1999 to deal with a predicted passenger growth of thirty-five million annually by the year 2005. Since those plans were made, the rate of development, following China's admission to the World Trade Organisation in 2001 and increased foreign interest, has outstripped these modest expectations. By 2002, despite extensions, the original airport site was considered inadequate for the newly-projected passenger figures over the next two decades. CAAC, the Civil Aviation Administration of China, were commissioned to carry out a feasibility study on the construction of a new airport.

By 2004 the publication *Airline Industry Information* announced that the Beijing Capital International Airport Co. had decided to construct a new runway as part of the preparations for the 2008 Olympics. A 19.45-billion-Yuan expansion plan would also include a new terminal building and cargo zone, along with auxiliary projects to enable the airport to deal, annually, with sixty million passengers and 1.8 million tones of cargo by the year 2015. The financial plan was approved in September 2003 and the subsequent first phase of the construction had to be completed, ready for trial runs in 2007, before the start of the Games.

Meanwhile an international competition for Passenger Terminal 3 had narrowed the competitors down to three: Foster and Partners with Arup and the Dutch airport planner NACO, the U.S. practice Yang Mowlem, and the French ADP. In a final stage these three consortiums were asked in October 2003 to scale down their proposals to an overall area of 350,000 square metres following a Chinese Government investigation into available financial resources. Savings were partially achieved by reducing the size of the terminal building and the intervals between gates.

In November 2003 Foster and Partners, Arup Engineers and NACO, who had proved their abilities at Chep Lap Kok, Hong Kong's International Airport, won the £1.2 billion contract for Beijing's Terminal 3. It is the world's biggest airport building project. To get a feel for it's size imagine all four London Heathrow terminals, plus another 25% capacity, under a single roof.

Terminal 3, located between the existing eastern runway and future third runway, as the visitor's first view on China, is planned to be a dramatic introduction to the newly modernized capital. Efficiency and sophisticated technology are to be the hallmarks of the development and despite its mammoth size the terminal has tried to achieve maximum passenger comfort with as few level changes as possible, short walking distances and quick transfer times. The hangar-like volume will be a fully glazed and airy space, bathed in daylight, with changing light effects to measure a pedestrian's progress through the building.

Passive and active building services are state-of-the-art; south-east orientated skylights to maximize the heat of the early morning sun, and integrated environmental control systems to minimize energy consumption and carbon emissions. A modular structure has been planned to enable the fast-track construction programme to meet the 2007 opening date. Key planning aims have been short term minimal disturbance for ongoing airport operations during construction and long term design flexibility to accommodate future growth.

Even in this hi-tech structure the architects have bowed to perceived traditional cultural sensibilities; the roof is described as a dragon's wing and colours in the building are to be primarily Chinese red and yellow.

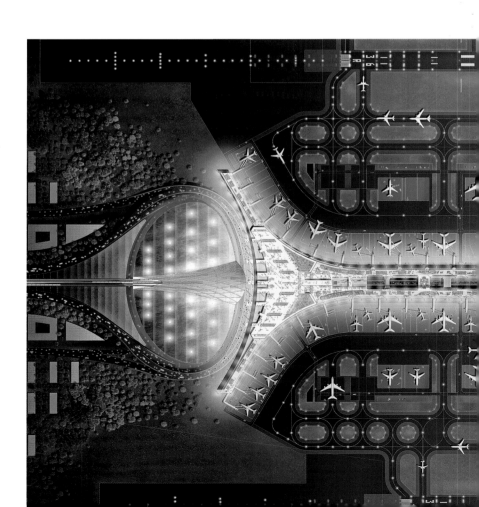

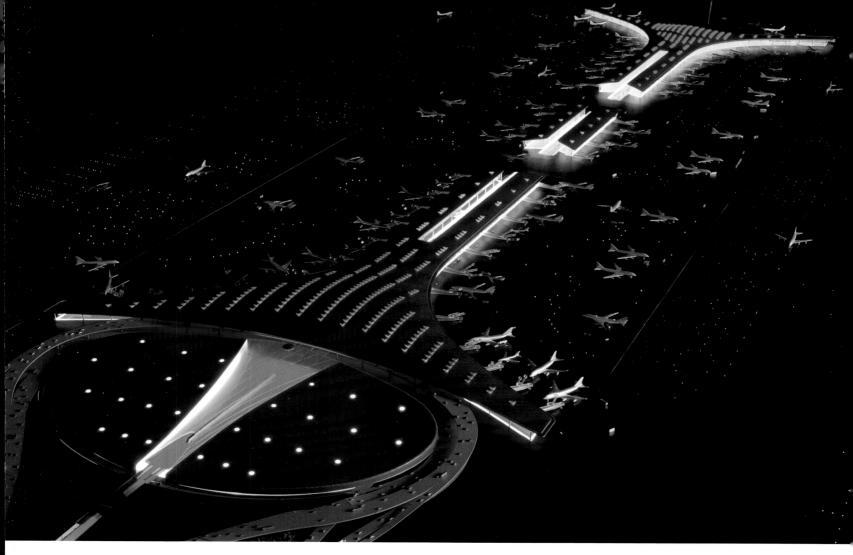

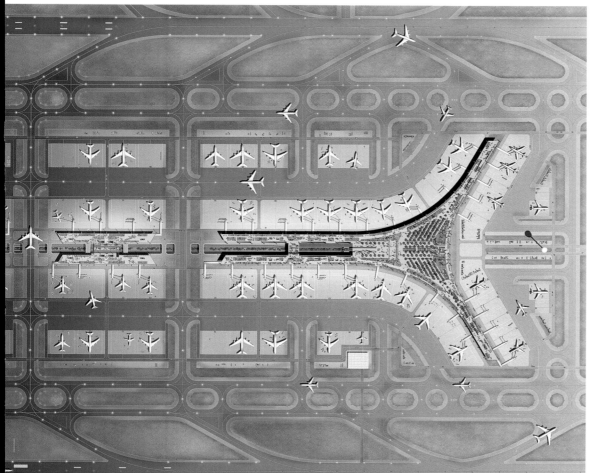

△ The dragon at night

◁ Terminal 3, docking and runway layout

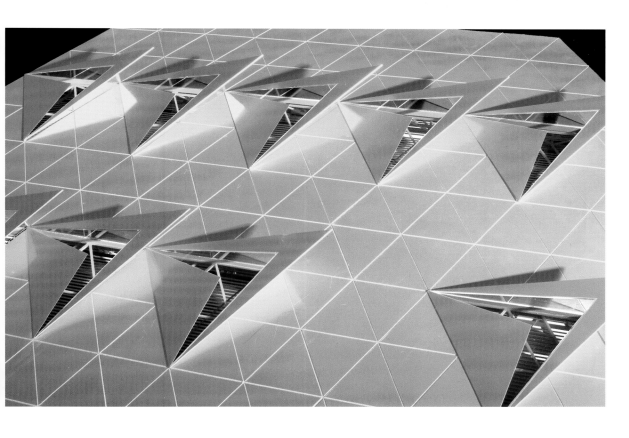

## one

◁ Red and yellow are China's
national colours

△ Roof apertures like gills

▽ Undulating dragon wing roofs

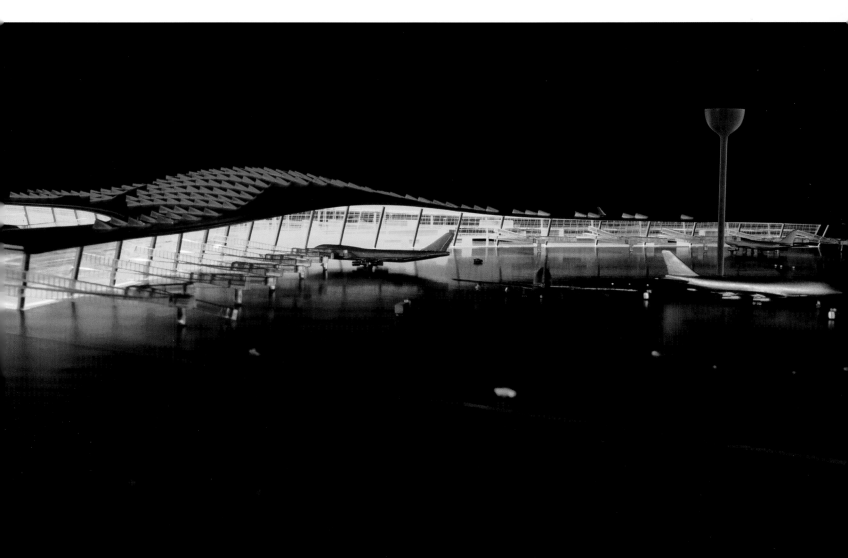

Zaha Hadid with Patrik Schumacher

# SOHO CITY MASTERPLAN, BEIJING

Planned 2003

Beijing municipality, covering roughly the area of Belgium, is constructed in rings of development encircling the Imperial Forbidden City and the living and working compound, Zhongnanhai, of the present rulers.

The capitals mosaic of historic, one-family settlements, once built right up to the edges of the Forbidden City, is giving way to modern commercial, cultural, shopping, entertainment and sports complexes and citizens are being moved out to new urban dormitories. With their monotonous monoculture these purely residential areas, springing up along the concentric highways, are long-term threats to the capital's metropolitan potential. This master plan uses a vocabulary, unknown as yet in China, to conjure up a twenty-first-century networked and serviced style 'SOHO', a technologically elite living and working, mixed-use sub-centre which could attain its own independent dynamic.

The inspiration and business acumen behind this idea is the husband and wife team of Pan Shiyi and Zhang Xin, who set up SOHO China. They first made their name with the Commune by the Great Wall project, for which they won an award at the 2002 Venice Biennale.

SOHO City's 35.2 hectare site, on the south-east corner of the Fourth Ring, is strategically placed near the planned exhibition centre in the Beijing Logistic Port. 800,000 square metres of gross floor area are to be arranged in an asymmetrical 'swarming' mass of tower blocks, some banana-shaped in plan, asymmetrically curved and rounded. The urban geometry of mixed functions should have nothing staid or stiff about its form. Architectural antecedents are the loft area of Manhattan, and similar developments in Japan and the West, where highly qualified and creative workers are able to design their own lifestyle and working rhythms. Fluid City is used to describe this development of unstructured green oases, home-office, exhibition and logistics centres rising in height and density towards a traffic crossing within the site boundaries.

The planning philosophy, to generate unity from diversity and urban intensity relieved by moments of intimacy, is not entirely new. Beijing's *hutongs*, grid lanes of courtyard housing, of which there were still 3,000 in the late eighties, are older than Manhattan lofts. With their private walled gardens, living quarters and craftsmen's workshops only separated by walls and cobbled yards from shops and schools, they were the feudal equivalent of today's integrated lifestyles which are only affordable in China by double income couples with no children. Only the technology and terminology have changed. The question as to whether such a vibrant community can be produced from a barren site remains open.

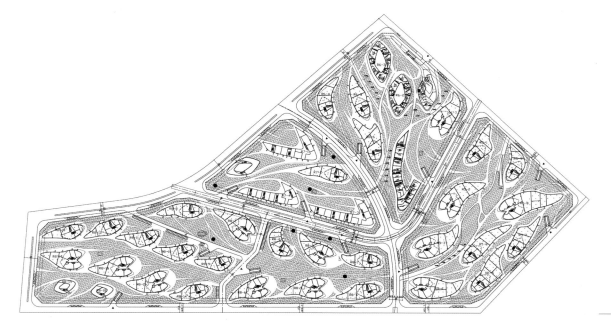

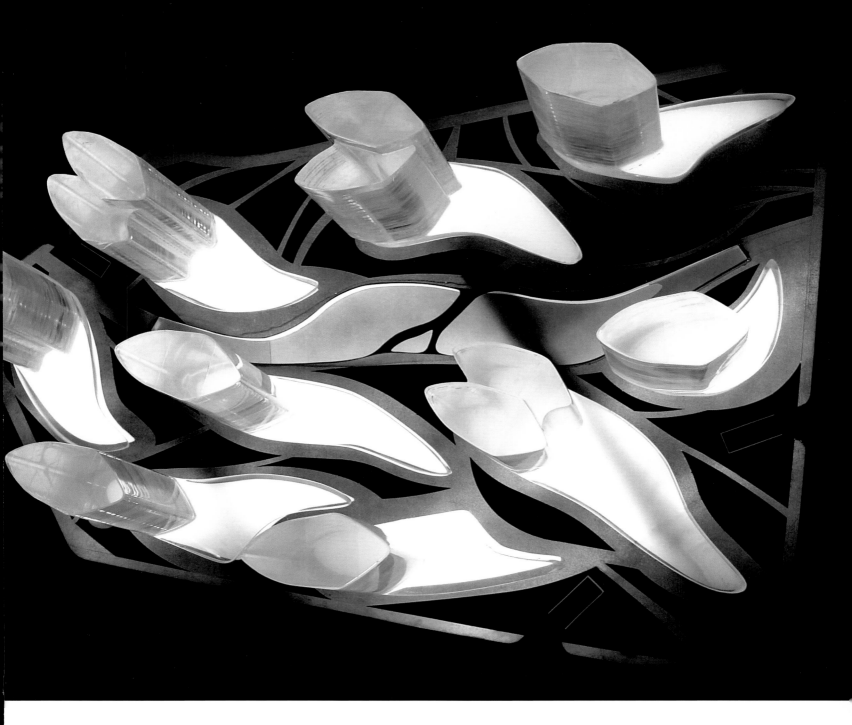

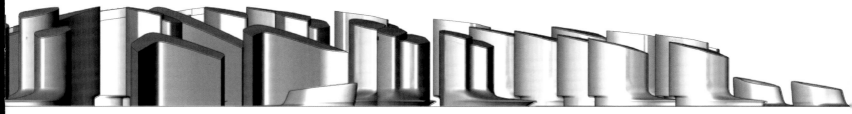

◁ SOHO City's 352 hectare site

△ Towers like tadpoles swimming across the landscape

▽ To combat monotony development rises to a peak height-limit

Kohn Pedersen Fox Associates

# HUA MAO CENTRE MASTERPLAN, BEIJING

Completion 2005

This is an effort to create a lively, mixed use district on a brown field site on the east side of the capital. With 144,600 square metres of shopping, 250,000 square metres of offices, an 82,700-square-metre hotel and 238,000 square metres of private residential space, this qualifies as a full-blown suburb.

Located between the developing Central Business District to the west, an industrial site to the north-east, the main Jianguo Road and a planned new park to the south, the area is well knitted into a metropolitan context. The area has been divided into three zones; office towers to the south, shops and the hotel in the centre, and homes to the north nearest the Central Business District. So, although this is a mixed use site, the building functions are strictly segregated from one another. Retail, commercial and residential do not intermingle in any one block.

Offices on the southern edge are grouped in three towers, 180, 150 and 120-metres high. These distinguishing landmarks face on to Jianguo Road. The tallest tower, in combination with a new footbridge across Jianguo, is an introduction to the urban mass and dominates the view from the eastern approach to Beijing. The smallest tower is prominent on the south-west corner of the site and focuses the eye into the shopping plaza at the heart of the development.

Shopping is nowadays celebrated as an 'experience'. A galleria of units and a dramatic hotel façade embrace a circular public plaza with water features and a landscaped amphitheatre. Throughout the day and into the evening this space should be like a stage on which local residents, office workers and the shopping public, play their part in an ever changing scene. These areas of accessible 'luxury' are certainly much loved by teenagers as places to hang out in, even when they cannot afford to buy anything in the shops.

On the northern edge of the site private apartments are being placed in blocks and occasional towers on a tree lined boulevard which is the extension of the main access into the central business district.

As with all these newly created mega projects thousands of private cars, service and delivery vehicles have to be accommodated somewhere. Official policy is to build up a national motor industry and stimulate a home market. Possession of a driving license and private car, as a measure of status, wins out against ownership of only a bicycle although, ironically, the speed of inner city travel has decreased in proportion to the increase in cars. In the Hua Mao Centre 5,400 car-park places are being provided in three separate areas, above and below ground.

▽ **left** Beijing's increasing proliferation of squares and grids, but on a larger scale than the former *hutongs*
**right** Regular and orderly rows of towers

△ A rhythm of towers and podiums
▽ Connected by asymmetrical lower level blocks and bridges

# CENTRAL AXIS MASTERPLAN, BEIJING

Study 2002–2003

It is not often that an architectural and planning office is approached to suggest an urban plan for 100 square metres in the centre of an existing capital city. This was the task AS&P were asked to take on in 2002. The area in question is Beijing's central north-south axis stretching over twenty-five kilometres, containing the most important historical and contemporary religious and political buildings. At the heart is the Forbidden City, home to the Ming and the Qing dynasties, which was laid out between 1406 and 1420 with, it is said, the help of a million labourers. The present structures are mainly post-eighteenth century. To the south is Tiananmen Square, flanked by Mao's Memorial Hall and National History Museum with the History of the Revolution. Zhongnanhai, to the west of the Imperial Forbidden City, is the residential and office compound of the present political elite. Planned as a pleasure ground for emperors between the tenth and thirteenth centuries, this compound was previously, between 1911 and 1949, the Presidential palace for the Republic of China. After 1949 communist leaders, Mao and Zhou Enlai among many others, lived and worked within the walls of this office park which also houses Party and Military headquarters. At all compass points around the Forbidden City parks were laid out as playgrounds and places for rituals performed by the emperors; Beihai Park, Temple of the Moon, Temple of the Earth, Agricultural Park, Temple of the Sun and Temple of Heaven parks.

The historic section of this Central Axis is roughly eight kilometres long. Extensions to the north and south have developed over the last few decades. The 2008 Olympics will be the focal centre of the North with the Olympic Green planned by Sasaki. For the more neglected southern section AS&P have proposed inserting a New Central Station as part of the national railway network, which would connect with the city's public transport network and may also become the location for the 'Transrapide' magnetic track system between Beijing and Shanghai. As a thriving transport hub and gateway to the capital the New Central Station would rejuvenate and give purpose to the area. In March 2005 Terry Farrell & Partners, in conjunction with the Tianjin Design Institute, won the international design competition for South Bejing's railway station to serve 400,000 passengers daily. North of the station a mixed use neighbourhood of commerce, shopping, and living accommodation, spread over ten square kilometres, should exemplify twenty-first-century energy-saving and non-polluting building technologies. South of the central station a six-square-kilometre Ecological Model City and Park is planned for experimental agriculture. The idea was to possibly make this 'green' experiment in living and working an external project of the 2010 Shanghai World Expo.

Satellite centres, each with clear goals, would relieve pressure on the historic centre and help improve the urban microclimate, with parks as green lungs to help break the dust-laden winds from the Gobi desert, and ecologically friendly building services. For the whole Central Axis solar power units, separation and recycling concepts for ground and rain water, the insertion of fresh air corridors, and a three kilometre wind energy park in the north, were suggested.

Searching for a cultural guideline the planners took the character 'Zhong', which means 'middle' or 'realm in the middle', as their inspiration. The square with a vertical brush stroke running through the centre sums up the order, symmetry and centralization, of China's traditional urban planning. Beijing, so far, has managed to retain its historic layout of grids and axis, set out according to the 'Guan Zi' or 'Kao Gong Ji' codes, defining relationships between urban and agricultural use, and building type forms. The development idea is to produce types of 'city modules' which can be plugged into an adaptable infrastructure network. This could be seen as a rehabilitation of the traditional form for twenty-first-century use. Traffic grids of 415 square metres match the ideal size of a classical city district. Sites within these grids have a depth of fifty-seventy metres, corresponding to the traditional *hutong* dimensions.

**The hierarchy of the north-south axis**

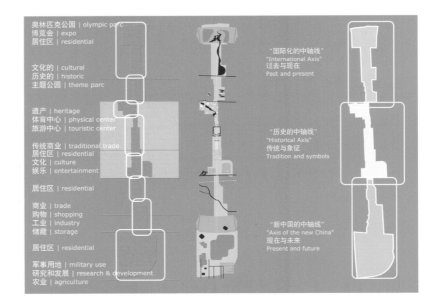

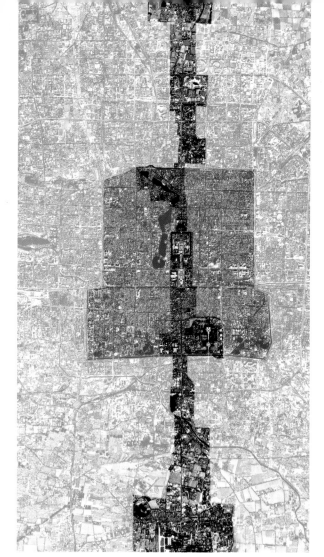

A twenty-five-kilometre cut through the heart of the Middle Kingdom introducing
business and transport nodes, with more urban green lungs

AS&P Albert Speer & Partner
# EXPO 2010 MASTERPLAN, SHANGHAI
Planned 2001

Following their experience as master planners for the German 2000 EXPO held in Hanover AS&P were asked in 2001 to prepare an urban development concept for Shanghai's EXPO 2010. The theme and motto is 'Better City, Better Life', linking China's rapid urban construction of the last few decades with the idea of a progressive quality of life for its citizens. With this leitmotif the master-plan foresees an EXPO designed as a model city district within the existing metropole. Forty million visitors are expected to attend the event and in preparation a 420-hectare, green field site was reserved on both sides of the Huangpu River, south of the city centre. The main focus of events will take place on the southern bank, spreading into new city suburbs and parks on the north bank which will gradually infiltrate the existing Shanghai layout as an 'Open Expo' development reaching into the city.

Interconnected EXPO areas include pavilion zones, the theme park, recreation and service areas, hotel accommodation and administrative centres. The design proposal offered various design solutions for the entrance zones and site access points, calculated parking needs and studied internal transportation options. The high point of the design is the Huangpu Plaza as a central public gathering point with a 'Spiral Tower' symbolizing the 'Better City, Better Life' theme.

In line with an officially proclaimed awareness of sustainable development the consequent post-EXPO use of the site is an important aspect of the proposal. Shanghai's advantage, in contrast to Germany's, is that an expanding economy should easily be able to absorb and find new uses for EXPO buildings and infrastructure in the growing urban fabric.

As so often happens in China the client has, since the original commission, revised the brief. The site has been enlarged and another architect has completed a master plan which, since 2004, has been incorporated in the Shanghai Urban Planning model on view in the Exhibition Centre in Peoples Park. There is still time, however, for the client to change his mind once more and decisions on the final form remain fluid.

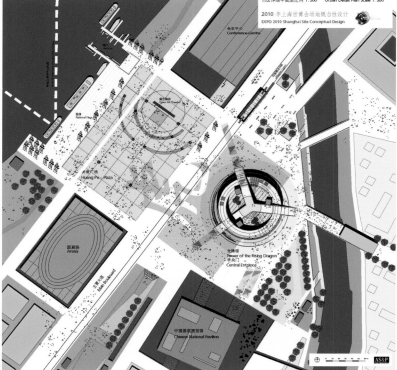

△ Aerial view of the southern bank looking north towards Shanghai city centre

**1 Section 1** scale 1 : 1.250

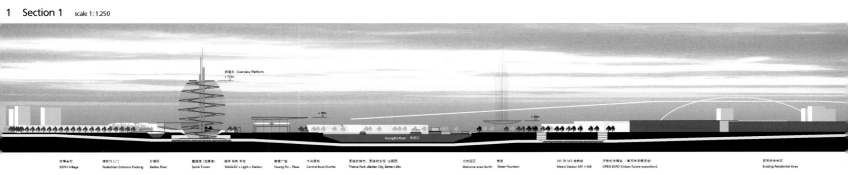

| 世博会村 | 浦东行人门 | 白莲河 | 螺旋塔（龙腾塔） | 磁浮 轻轨，车站 | 黄浦广场 | 中央渡轮 | 更绿的城市，更佳的生活 主题园 | 北侧迎区 | 喷泉 | M5 和 M8 地铁站 | 开放式市博会（都市未来博览会） | 现有的住宅区 |
| EXPO-Village | Pedestrian Entrance Pudong | Bailian River | Spiral Tower | MAGLEV + Light + Station | Huang Pu - Plaza | Central Boat-Shuttle | Theme Park »Better City, Better Life« | Welcome area North | Water Fountain | Metro-Station M5 + M8 | OPEN EXPO (Urban future exposition) | Existing Residential Area |

# BANK OF CHINA HEAD OFFICE, BEIJING

Completed 2001

The China Bank's headquarters in Beijing could not avoid being monumental and impressive. The choice of architect, an internationally known American of Chinese origins with historical family connections to the bank in pre-1949 Shanghai, was also an inevitable gesture. Located in Xidan, one underground stop to the west of Tiananmen Square, in a district now denuded of any historical buildings but crowded, as far as the eye can see, with department stores covered in garish advertising amid motorized mayhem, the bank block looks less impressive than it did on completion. Walking through its halls visitors might imagine they are in an Egyptian mausoleum. The volumes are pyramids in negative with cliff-like walls merging with floors and terraces of smooth cream stone.

The building, which conforms with Beijing's 13.7-metre building height limit, has a floor area of 170 thousand square metres for 2,500 employees, a twenty-four-hour foreign exchange trading room, high-tech global network control centre, monumental banking halls, reception hall, and employee's services. The thirty-metre, square, 2,000-seat auditorium or multi-functional hall, with a 6.5-metre ceiling, is a column-free space in which media presentations are possible in eight languages with simultaneous translation. Basement parking was designed for 500 cars and bicycles.

A Travertine-clad envelope was chosen to mask the yellow Gobi Desert dust which blows regularly over the capital, and its square solidity around the perimeter follows Beijing's tradition of impenetrable façades to the street which open internally on to landscaped courts. These are public plazas, offering short-cuts across the city block and shelter from hot summers and winter winds, but their appearance is intimidating and too perfect to be welcoming. Hangzhou bamboos, over fifteen metres high, form screens around the courtyards where decorative rocks from the Stone Forest National Park in Yunnan Province stand in shallow pools filled with goldfish. Water symbolizes wealth and fish good luck

As a seminal work in the capital many of the construction techniques, which were new to China, raised standards and expectations for later projects. Four fifty-five-metre steel trusses, forming a two-storey box girder structure around the perimeter, were the largest ever constructed in China. Unfortunately they were clad to be made more representational, not left exposed to show the clarity of construction. The atrium's German-manufactured, fifty-metre, square skylight, consisting of a series of glazed pyramids, was assembled on the roof of the building in four modules which were then moved on tracks across the roof opening to be bolted together. This technique avoided using scaffolding and allowed construction to continue below. No expense was spared either on the fitting out. A unique flexible workstation furniture system, designed in Canada, was manufactured in China for the bank's thirty departments.

In the banking halls a suspended, spoked ring of lights was inspired by Beijings plethora of bikes. Nowadays this has an almost historical symbolism and is yet another example of how fast China has moved. The Bank headquarters was one of only four architectural projects of national importance chosen in 1999 to celebrate the fiftieth anniversary of the People's Republic.

▽ **Mammoth city blocks dwarf the few trees or patches of park**

▷ **The foyer is an oasis of meticulously placed natural and manmade objects**

An artificial landscape of Yunnan's aesthetically eroded and highly prized rocks, combined with pools, bamboos, and dramatic day and night lighting, recalls an ancient intellectual pursuit of garden design

# CCTV CENTRAL CHINESE TELEVISION HEADQUARTERS, BEIJING

Completion 2008

OMA's 6,000 million Yuan headquarters for CCTV has been rightly described as mammoth. This project will be the first of 300 tower structures already in the planning pipeline for Beijing's new Central Business District. The complex with two major buildings will cover four city blocks between Chang'an Avenue and the Third Ring Road. The total of 553,000 square metres of useable space will be twice the size of previous projects by OMA, who won the commission against ten other U.S., Japanese and European international architects. The continuously writhing form, like an angular snake, will be a prominent example of a new generation of designs, in which the classical twentieth-century's articulation and separation of form and content, structure and non-load bearing skin, no longer apply. Functions lock together, like a Chinese three-dimensional wooden puzzle, forming a network of interrelated departments in the broadcasting organization. The architects, calling this a communal circulation loop, have convinced the client that this form of planning will help interdepartmental communication. Here the idea of the 'collective' is translated from communism to capitalism for increased efficiency among a work force of 10,000.

The two structures on the eighteen hectare site will be the CCTV headquarters, 230 metres high with a total of 575,000 square metres of floor area for administration, broadcasting, studios and program production, and the TVCC Television Cultural Centre, a 52,000-square-metre block with hotel, visitor's centre, public theatre and exhibition spaces. A Media Park landscape, for outdoor filming, public entertainment and more production studios, will knit the two buildings together and becomes an extension of the central green axis of the Central Business District. Unlike the skyscrapers born in Chicago and New York these are not vertically thrusting pinnacles but asymmetrical, sensuous loops with criss-crossing skin markings, to visually highlight the structural forces at work.

Rem Koolhaas is one of the few western architects who has optimistically and enthusiastically embraced the challenge of building in China with a philosophy reconnecting technology and progress. This breaks with pessimistic or anxious attitudes prevalent in older developed countries, especially in Europe, where new applied sciences, notably in the fields of automation, nuclear power or genetic research, have not been seen as automatically serving human social progress.

Here, taking advantage of a *tabula rasa* situation, a young and unfettered marketing revolution and the wish of China's

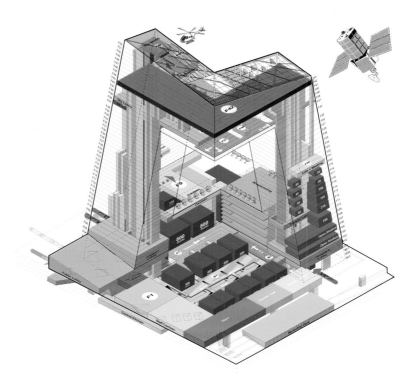

clients to outdo the west, the architects have pushed out the envelope of design possibilities and tested client acceptance with projects which would be hard to complete elsewhere. Along with the CCTV, and TVCC, OMA also won in January 2004 the competition for the £42-million ($80-million) Beijing Books Building.

In May 2004, when the CCTV was ready to start on site, there was an unexpected delay in obtaining approval for construction. China's Prime Minister Wen Jiabao and President Hu Jintao, who had been in power for a year, had promised to deal with the overheating of the economy, amid fears of inflation, and the unequal distribution of the country's newly created affluence. Many mega-projects were put on hold awaiting a survey and review of their budgets. Since then it has been reported that design and construction will continue.

△ **A Chinese puzzle**

▷ **A distinctive silhouette among the conforming stiff backed towers of contemporary Beijing**

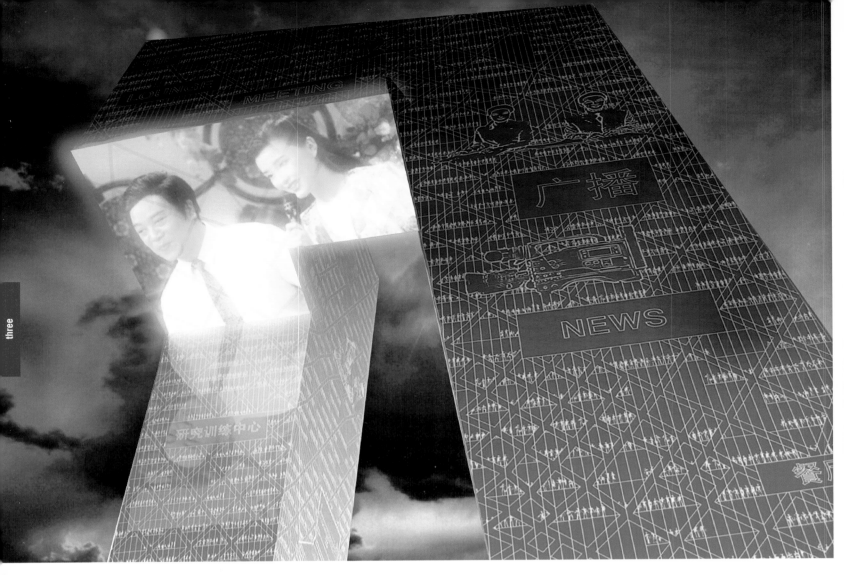

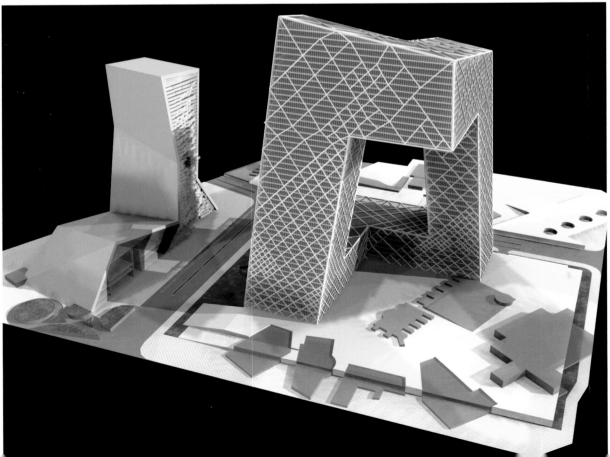

# POLICE HEADQUARTERS, SHUNDE

Completion 2005

Shunde City has become one of the most affluent areas on the mainland during the last two decades, very much due to its proximity to Hong Kong, the establishment of the Special Economic Zone, and the oil drilling which first started in the Pearl Estuary. It has achieved continuous double figures in annual economic growth.

Moving from a state controlled economy to free market capitalism with the accompanying movement of population, new business ventures and a construction boom, has produced more legislation, laws and regulations, necessitating more control. In all Chinese cities security forces, traffic wardens, police and the army are conspicuously present in every street. Police centres are only one of a range of recently modernised institutional and state organizations for which new premises have to be provided.

In Shunde New City centre the police have a strategic 35,000-square-metre corner site in a district set aside for government buildings. The seventeen-storey administration tower sits on a four-storey podium containing a convention centre, training facilities, indoor swimming pool, canteen and dormitory. Like soldiers, the police live on the premises too. The building's gross floor area is 52,000 square metres and there is an additional 20,000 square metres of basement car parking.

Appropriately for a semi-military establishment the main entrance to the tower block is symbolized by an impressively dimensioned, modern equivalent of the military gateway tower on the Great Wall. Building elements are arranged in layers, running parallel to each other, like curtains through which one has to pass to reach the centre. A rational façade grid with deep reveals and embedded masonry framed windows will produce interesting and changing light effects during the course of the day and also function as louvers against the sun's glare. A filigree effect has tried to soften what could have been a heavy fortress design while maintaining, by the size and height of the project, an imposing and representational face to the public. Although still forbidding this new building type at least breaks with the traditional Chinese police garrison and barracks form.

▽  **Symmetrical planning in which balance and counter-balance are valued traditions**

▷  **The building as a huge portal, the modern equivalent of military towers on the Great Wall**

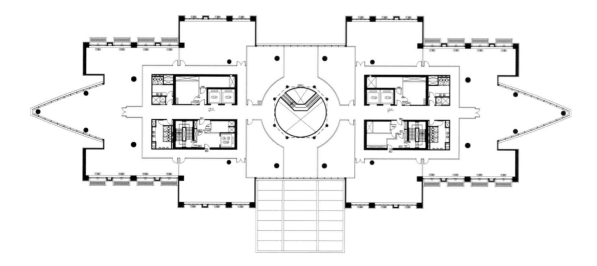

Kohn Pedersen Fox Associates

# CHINA NATURAL OFFSHORE OIL CORPORATION HEADQUARTERS, BEIJING

In construction

Asia Money magazine voted China's Natural Offshore Oil Corporation, CNOOC, the best managed Chinese company in 2001. The previous year it had a total revenue of 27.6 billion RMB, of which a third was profit. Its corporate arms are geographically wide spread and encompass branch offices in Tianjin, Zhanjiang, Shenzhen and Shanghai, an overseas office in Singapore, four research, engineering and shipping companies, five logistic companies, four oil, petrochemical, gas and power companies, along with five investment, finance and oilfield service companies. Corporation history started in 1967 with the first offshore well drilled in the Bohai Gulf. Since then it has explored and set up wells all around the Chinese coast.

Located in Beijing's Dongcheng district, at a major crossing on the capital's Second Ring Road, the eighteen-storey CNOOC headquarters is an equal visual weight to the Ministry of Foreign Affairs building on the opposite corner. It is a tailored project for a specific client to match the unique significance of this corporation which deals with some of the nation's most important natural resources. The architects have chosen an easily read picture book narrative with shapes hinting at the prow of an oil tanker, a tower like an off shore oil rig superstructure, and the ground floor finish suggesting a watery surface.

The rotated triangular tower maximizes the use of the site and creates an entrance through a courtyard along the quieter side of the block. A symbolic gateway quotes Beijing's traditional, and now rapidly disappearing, historical, courtyard housing form. The problem of bringing light into the core is solved by sky gardens which cut away sections of the floor to allow daylight into the atrium on three sides. An L-shaped podium containing communal function rooms, such as meeting and conference facilities, public restaurants and exhibition spaces on three levels, forms the perimeter to this internal and semi-private open space with its fountain, water features and planting designed by consultants from the Beijing Botanical Gardens. Like an iceberg two thirds of the built area, 65,000 square metres, are above ground while the 29,000 square metres below ground are service areas for storage, plant rooms and parking.

▽ **The smoothly curved triangular tower dominates the city block**

▷ **Architecture like the prow of an oil tanker**

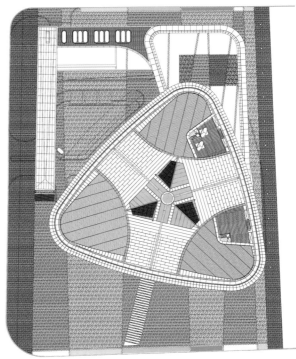

◁ Looking down into
the open well of the tower

△ Ground level foyer
▽ Section showing standard
underground parking levels,
podium block and gently raked
tower façade

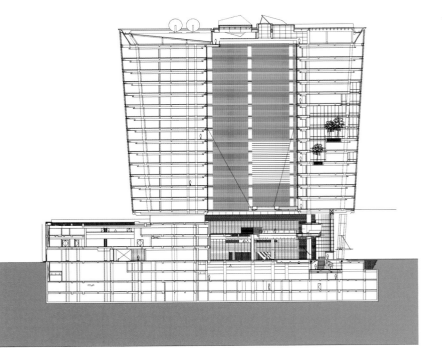

# CHINA PETRO HEADQUARTERS, BEIJING

2003 International competition 1st prize

The global business of this national organization is reflected in the size and quality of the architectural design and the importance of its location on Beijing's 2nd Ring road. Running parallel to one of the highly trafficked, fast-moving, loud and dusty, multi-lane roads which forms part of the race track system feeding the capital's corporate business headquarters, the functions of this 180,000-square-metre building could very well have been encapsulated in an hermetically sealed envelope. Instead of closing in on itself, however, the building reacts to the street scene, extenuating the direction given by the Ring road and rising in height to mark a major crossing and also adds variation with setbacks, overhangs, colour and voyeur glimpses into the workspaces, for the interest of the passing public.

The block is broken into two connected bodies—a low and long, twelve-storey structure at the north end of the site and a prominent twenty-three-storey slab on the south side. The preliminary competition design shows an attempt to break the monolithic scale with finely fenestrated glass shells containing further boxes-within-a-box, while the perimeter has been given irregularities of line and five voids have been hollowed out from the structural body of the building. The alternating sequence of enclosed working spaces and garden-like volumes sets up a Yin and Yang rhythm of contrasts and balances. With the site fully covered, right up to the pavement line, there was no free buffer zone for a green border to soften the building's hard-edged profile. These internal atriums, each several storeys high and flooded with daylight or artificially illuminated at night, offer an alternative which can be appreciated by both office workers and public. Each garden is dedicated to one of the five continents in which the Petro conglomerate is active and also takes on the characteristics of one of the five elements—earth, fire, water, metal and wood, which form the basis of Feng Shui and Chinese horoscope composition, the placing of objects in harmony with each other.

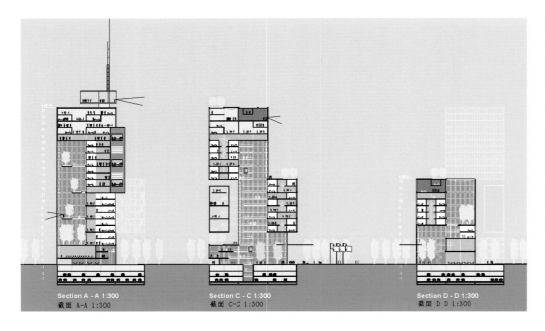

Section A - A 1:300
截面 A-A 1:300

Section C - C 1:300
截面 C-C 1:300

Section D - D 1:300
截面 D D 1:300

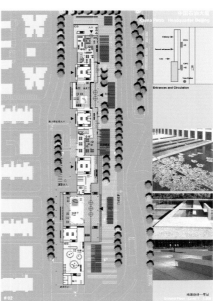

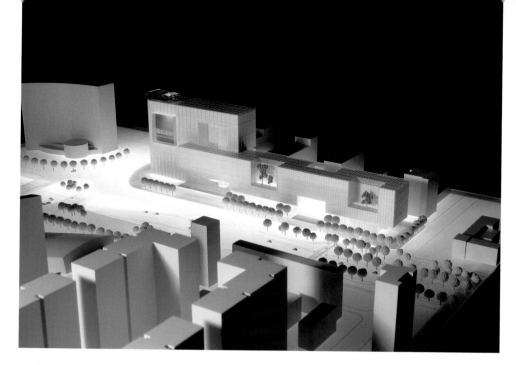

◁ left  Sections of boxes-within-boxes
right  Site plan

▷  Although hemmed in by express highways
the architecture has created various sizes of
internal gardens as dust and pollution barriers
and to oxygenate the micro climate

Dennis Lau & Ng Chun Man

# CITIC PLAZA,
# TIEN HO, GUANGZHOU

Completed 1995

Tien Ho, as a new city suburb, has been planned on a grand scale with forty-metre-wide boulevards and the formality of the CITIC Plaza design responds to this town planning approach of symmetry and landmark structures used as punctuation to views. A line drawn between the CITIC tower, Guangzhou's main railway station, the East Station and the Tien Ho Sports stadium defines the city's main north-south axis, and the CITIC is one of the first structures the visitor sees when arriving by train.

In the early eighties CITIC was already internationally active as the exploratory investment arm of the People's Republic, gathering experience and making forays into the global market, especially in Hong Kong which provided China with a quick course in capitalism. In preparing the economic basis for China's present activities it had a pioneering role which deserved a pioneering structure.

When completed in 1995 this was the tallest, reinforced concrete building in the world at 390 metres. The complex consists of three vertical elements; two blocks of serviced apartments and an eighty-storey office tower, rising from a semi-circular podium containing a three-level shopping mall. The apartments look down on to the roof of the podium which is landscaped as a private communal garden with swimming pool.

To keep costs down and help support China-based industries, the external finishes, curtain walling, glazed ceramic tiles, and anodized aluminium framed windows were virtually all locally sourced. Size and compactness of the planning also helped reduce capital construction costs and on-going maintenance costs which the architects claim are low per unit area. The lines are modern and the tower has elegant proportions. Apart from its brief historical engineering fame the base and towers format, structural design and architectural detailing, are reminiscent of many standard Hong Kong mixed use projects and would be equally at home in the U.S. or Singapore. When this was being designed and built, however, this stringency, which avoided superfluous and inappropriate ethnic emblems, was praiseworthy. At the same time many other contemporary foreign architects were resorting to a neo-Chinese styling in the hope of finding favour with their mainland Chinese clients.

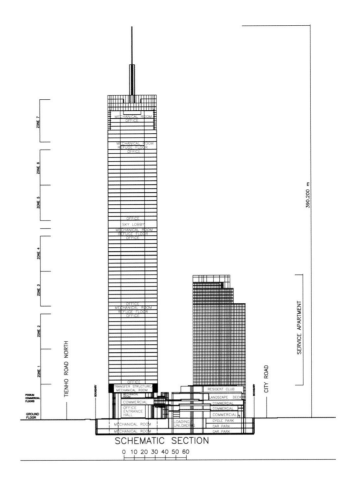

SCHEMATIC SECTION

0 10 20 30 40 50 60

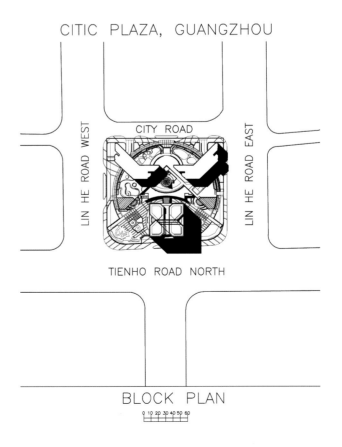

CITIC PLAZA, GUANGZHOU

BLOCK PLAN

0 10 20 30 40 50 60

△ Section through the two structures
▽ An integral city block of towers,
plaza and formal gardens

▷ Powerfully impressive symmetry

Foster and Partners

# JIUSHI CORPORATION HEADQUARTERS, SHANGHAI

Completed 2001

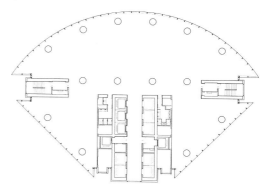

▽ The Jiushi tower is the highest building on the, as yet, underdeveloped southern end of the Bund overlooking the Huangpu River

▽ The Jiushi tower is the highest building on the, as yet, underdeveloped southern end of the Bund overlooking the Huangpu River

This building has a special status as the first project completed by a British firm of architects on mainland China after 1949. In 2002 it won the Lu Ban Chinese construction industry prize. Every year building companies celebrate Lu Ban day with banquets to which they invite associated consultants and sub-contractors. Born in 606 B.C. Lu Ban is considered the patron saint of all construction although he himself was, what would now be called, a joiner or carpenter. He is reputed to be China's first woodwork master. Foster and Partners had already completed the Hong Kong Bank headquarters, and Hong Kong's Chek Lap Kok Airport, as a replacement for Kai Tak Airport, before and after the colony's reunification with the People's Republic in 1997.

The Jiushi Corporation, important Chinese investors in Shanghai's development, chose to locate their headquarters on a prominent site at 28, Zhong Shan Nan Road, on the corner of Dong Men Road, overlooking the Huangpu River, the historical Bund, and the new business Pudong district. The forty-storey, 168-metre-high tower with 62,000 square metres of floor area, elliptical curved façade for maximum panoramic river views and column free interiors, was Foster and Partners 1994 winning design in an international competition. Several unique features of the design set this skyscraper apart from the general mass of American style towers which were being built and designed in the first Shanghai rush.

At the time it was the first Chinese building to use a triple skin ventilated glazing system allowing maximum daylight penetration without internal solar over heating. The transparency of the cladding does not block building users external views and also highlights the outsiders view of the building's basic

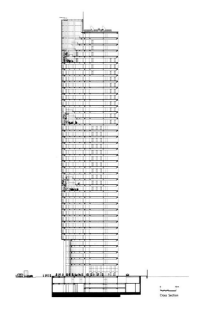

◁ **Enclosed garden atriums under the elliptical glass roof**

▷ **Until now a solitary giant in the colonial Chinese Quarter of Shanghai**

floor plates and column structure. The slender vertical, nearly invisible, glazing frames are part of the highly engineered cladding system, co-designed with Permasteelisa Spa of Italy and shipped pre-assembled to Shanghai for installation on site. The outer double glazed unit has heat-soak tested, toughened glass and an internal back-up wall of clear toughened glass that can be opened. Depending on orientation each façade has slightly different glazing. The north façade has low-emissive, coated glass. On the south-east and south-west façades the double-glazed unit has a ventilated cavity to prevent internal heat build-up. Air trapped in the cavity rises naturally as it heats up and is expelled at the top of the building making way for cooler air to be drawn in at the base. This Brownian motion continually cools the glazing. Motorized perforated Venetian blinds for shade and glare control are sandwiched between the double glazed units and the internal back-up wall.

Another unique feature for Shanghai's contemporary generation of towers was the six-storey, glazed, winter garden. Like their American models most tower roof-tops are reserved for air-conditioning, tanks and other service rooms. On three of the forty levels the floors are stepped back to form enclosed terraces, ideal for large gatherings. The adjacent six-storey block of shops, restaurants and bars, relates to the street line with a double height colonnade reminiscent of Shanghai's historical shopping arcades.

The underlying concept for the Jiushi Tower is, however, not so much a result of the Chinese context but the architects work over many decades on multi-storey projects in both Europe and Asia. Common features are the emphasis on reduced energy

consumption and the so-called 'European office' in which building users are all given external views and more spacious planning. This includes the insertion of sky gardens, to oxygenate the air and as recreational spaces, double height or higher atriums to relieve the monotony of volumes and give psychological 'room to breathe'. Internal communication is also encouraged by clear sight lines across floors, achieved by moving the service core away from the centre of the plan, and permitting views of floors above and below through the atrium volumes. Varying volumes, setbacks and sky gardens, all help to subtly break up the uncompromising and aggressive sleekness of a traditional skyscraper but, whereas in Europe the planted areas are left open, and naturally ventilated, Shanghai's humid climate requires enclosed winter gardens. Orientation of the building and floor planning all aim to take advantage of the city's spectacular skyline. Two triangular sections on the tower's south and west look out, respectively, on to the Nan Pu Bridge and the Yuyuan Gardens, and the T-shaped concrete core is positioned on the only side of the tower where wider views are blocked by an existing hotel. Aluminium panels, as external expressions of the individual floor plates, reflect lighting conditions in the sky during the day, and the red and yellow internal walls of the lift lobby and escape stairs appear as illuminated vertical strips at night.

An unfortunate result of the 'one world' market place has, however, meant that the building now suffers from a 'glazing sickness' which has broken out worldwide. The perimeter was cordoned off for safety in Autumn 2004 when a glazing unit fell to the street.

Kohn Pedersen Fox Associates

# WORLD FINANCIAL CENTRE, SHANGHAI

Completion 2007

When complete, the Shanghai World Financial Centre will be the world's tallest building, with 101 storeys rising 492 metres above ground level. In late 2004 it was still only a walled building site but, as a paper design, it had already received the New York American Institute of Architects 1995 Project Design Award. Situated at the centre of the Asian international banking district of Lujiazhui, in Pudong, the tower's monolithic simplicity and height are meant to underline Shanghai's status as a financial world heavyweight. It will stand, in solitary splendour, in its own city block next to SOM's 420-metre-high Jin Mao Tower, one of the world's tallest skyscrapers. The gradual change in floor plan and area from square podium to chisel like apex divides the tower's use from offices on the larger area lower levels to 300 smaller luxury hotel suites above. Guests will undoubtedly pay dearly for the superb view across the city.

Although described as incorporating characteristics of Chinese tradition the developer was in fact the Japanese property tycoon Minoru Mori, who joined forces with thirty-three Japanese banks, insurance and trading houses to invest 100 billion Yen, or 823 million US$. Starting as a square plan podium footprint the tower metamorphosis as it rises to end up as a blunt chisel with a fifty-metre hole. If the tower were a needle this cut out would be the giant eye. The square base corresponds to the earth, stable and symmetric, the change to a circle symbolizes heaven and the circular void is meant to represent the sun. This has not been without controversy. Some Chinese at first objected that this sun symbol, associated with the Japanese flag, was a provocation in a city which had suffered so much under Japanese occupation in World War II. The functional reason for the cut out is that it relieves wind pressure, and will therefore reduce structural movement during typhoons, at the top of the tower. There are said to have been plans for a Ferris wheel or big dipper within this void but, apart from the danger of terrorist action, the cost of normal safety precautions for such a public entertainment would seem to make this dream mere pie in the sky. There will however be an observation deck. Equal in diameter to the sphere of the Oriental Pearl TV Tower, only a few blocks away, the void is also meant to form a visual link between, what will be, the city's two most prominent landmarks. In reality only a bird flying 101 storeys above the street will have the perspective to match the TV orb with the Financial Centre's void. In its transformation from base to apex the tower also orientates itself to face the Oriental Pearl Tower in order to create the impression of two giants in dialogue across the sky.

Construction has progressed in fits and starts. Site work began in August 1997 but was suspended as a result of the Asian financial crisis. Five years later in 2003 construction was resumed. The 2001 September 11 terrorist attacks have also influenced the project design. There are specially designed shelters every twelve floors and large scale emergency facilities underground for use in the event of terrorist action, a fire or an earthquake.

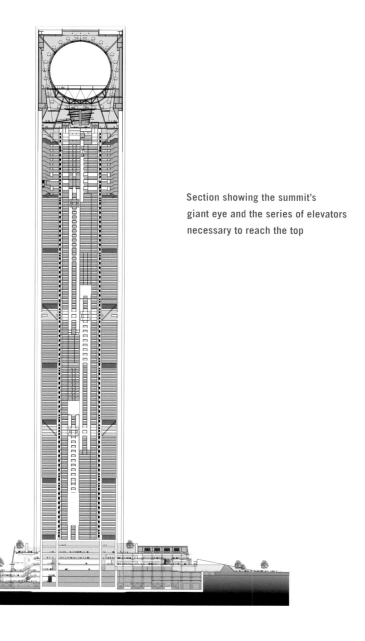

Section showing the summit's giant eye and the series of elevators necessary to reach the top

△ A grand entrance in keeping with the project's status

▽ The tower as chisel embedded in an abstract composition

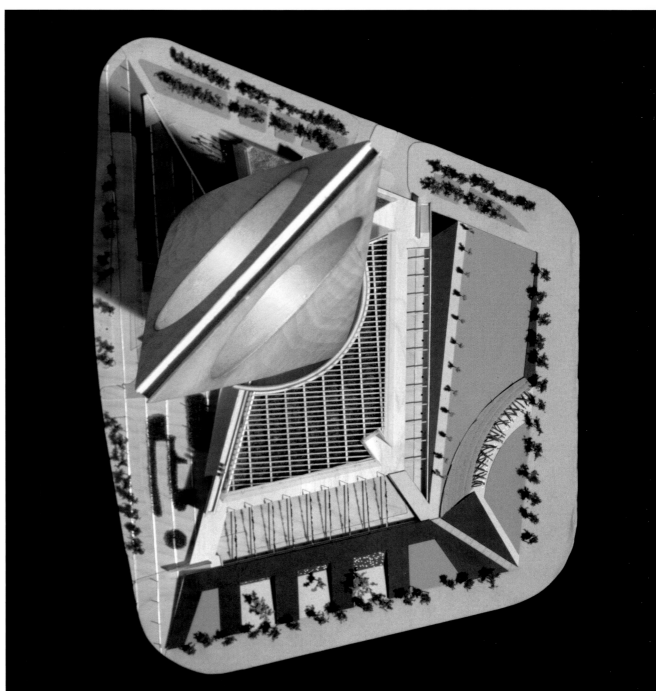

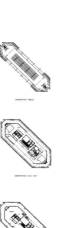

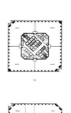

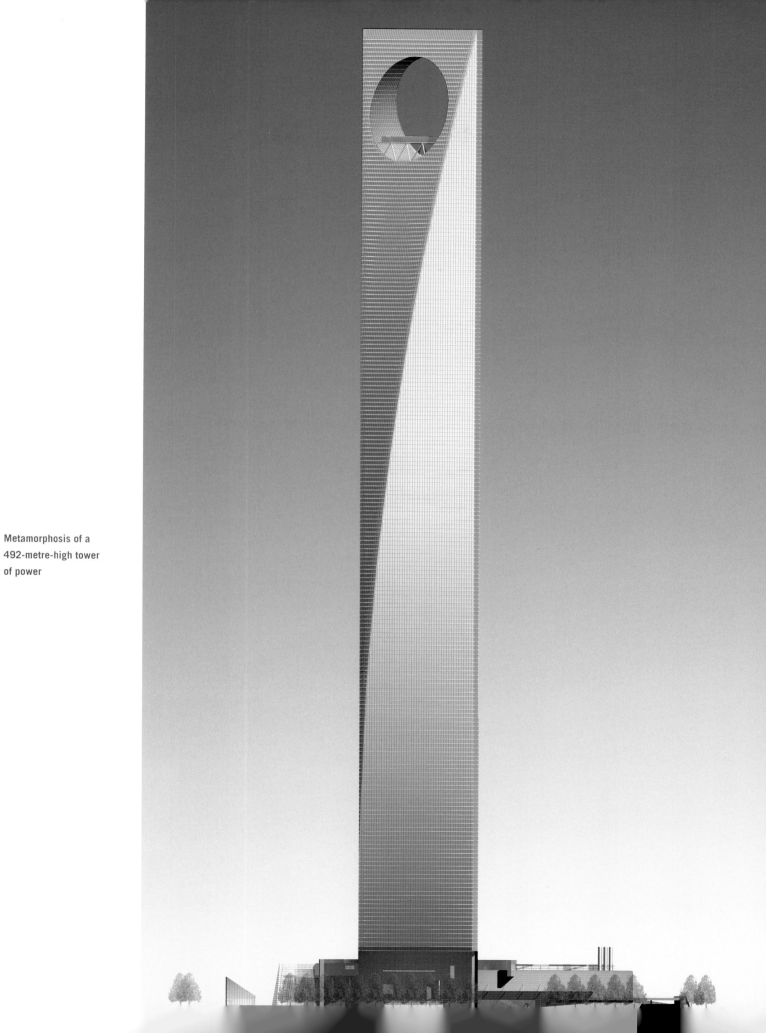

Metamorphosis of a
492-metre-high tower
of power

# SHOPPING MAZE, CENTRAL BUSINESS DISTRICT, WUXI S.E.Z.

Completed 2004

Why do cities have to be segregated into city blocks? asks Qingyun Ma. Under Capitalism, an urban fragment ringed by roads is a crude way to define legal ownership but people's lives, their work, duties and leisure, spill over borders and cannot be so easily segregated. In a Chinese city the concept of blocks has been adopted as a management convenience but it puts paid to any urban homogeneity and restricts the easy flow of activities. In a country where land is only leased from the state for a specific period, Qingyun Ma asks why town planning has to accept capitalist norms. In this project for Wuxi he took a Smithsonian urban ideal and challenged the notions of strictly defined city blocks. His hope is that, given the opportunities to experiment, Chinese architecture and planning may find structures which surpass previous, capitalist and socialist, systems.

Wuxi lies on the Jinghang Grand Canal, 128 kilometres West of Shanghai in Jiangsu province. It is one of China's oldest cities with a 3,000 year history and was once rich in tin, but the name 'Wuxi' means 'no tin' and began being used for the settlement before the Han period when the tin mines had already been exhausted. Since then the city has developed silk, pottery and brick industries. Nowadays visitors come to see the gardens and parks, the Lingshan Buddha and Turtle Head Island. Lake Taihu, which supports a fish industry, is also an attraction.

At first the client's brief was for unrelated commercial development on several separate plots in the centre of Wuxi. The architect suggested creating structures to connect and fuse the plots, the use of enclosed bridges over the river, access to the waterside, the inclusion into the scheme of abandoned sites and the selective demolition of obsolete structures. This was called a process of additive extraction, rather like pulling out rotten teeth to make way for new growth and holistic healing. The idea is to create an urban density of continuous space, melting together different movement flows, people's individual programmes and their daily experiences.

The reality is an architecture, covering a 159,210 square metre site, of colour and delight. Strong, visible, structural grids in modernist white style support panels of contrasting materials and overlapping uses. A zigzag route across the town interweaves both older blocks, not included in the development, pieces of industrial archaeology, and historical brick and terracotta buildings which have been lovingly restored for new functions.

◁ Unexpected treatment of the elevations

△ Pleasing contrasts between historical and modern forms without resorting to kitsch

A project of sufficient size to set new aesthetic standards without the arrogance of big gestures

# Y-TOWN, CENTRAL COMMERCIAL DISTRICT AND CULTURAL CENTRE, NINGBO

Completed 2004

Ningbo, 'calm waves', is an important economic centre and ocean going port, although it lies twenty kilometres inland at the junction of the Yuyao and Yong rivers. In the thirteenth century it was important for trade with Japan and Korea. Portuguese began using the harbour in the sixteenth century and, after the 1843 Opium War, Ningbo was ceded, under the first of several treaties obtained under duress, to the European traders as one of the treaty ports with a British Consulate.

Y-Town, with its commercial centre and museum in a former ferry terminal, is a complex 49,000 square metre site wedged between the river and a broad main road. Classified as an historical district the project, with two clients and several advisory consultants with conflicting and hard to reconcile aims, was one which Qingyun Ma admitted he would normally have tried to avoid. On the other hand it was an opportunity too good to miss which required the architects to be involved in basic and historical research, strategy, master planning and architectural design, through to interior design on the whole project.

Again the functional planning and architectural concept is one of collage. Historic grey brick buildings with traditional brown painted timber window frames and pantile roofs sit in juxtaposition to modern Miesian grey brick blocks with horizontal ribbon window slots. White Corbusian villa pilotis support white, flying roof terrace pavilions on ochre panelled buildings. Grey steel exposed I-beams support framed structures with large glazed areas alternating with enclosed sections. Earth tones and subtle shades of modern colours contrast with traditional Chinese chalk white plastered walls. Spatial relationships also play with contrast and surprise. Narrow pedestrian lanes open out on to broad riverside vistas and open public ways end in enclosed private gardens.

Ningbo was the architects first, major, successful project and, perhaps as a measure of its popularity, the cultural centre has become a favourite film location.

◁ In keeping with the historical urban scale

Traditional urban elements with modern in-fills

Kohn Pedersen Fox Associates

# PLAZA 66, NANJING XI LU, SHANGHAI

Phase I complete. Phase II under construction

The architects openly acknowledge the challenge of constructing two, sixty and forty-three-storey towers with a shopping mall right in the heart of Shanghai's old city centre. Nanjing Xi Lu is the historic former colonial business area of high-rise buildings fronting alleys and courtyards of old, derelict homes and restaurants. The refurbishment is still sometimes only skin deep. Where there were once hawkers and street food stalls competing with traffic there are now pedestrianised streets of fashion label boutiques and international chain stores.

The difference in scale between historic and new is startling. Plaza 66 has 93,000 square metres of office space in Tower I and 90,000 square metres in the second phase Tower II, also shopping and entertainment in the mall and below ground car parking. Supposedly the five storey podium, of 45,000 square metres, has been designed to match the scale of Nanjing Xi Lu, with smaller shop units in keeping with the bustle along the pedestrian way. Two large internal public areas, white clad and puristic with potted palms, are cut into the podium and embraced by the curved Tower I walls which rise to 281 metres. Against the night sky the top glass lantern level glows in the dark.

In contrast to the smaller scale, loud and lively, surrounding street life the boutiques in the Plaza remain quiet. The image might be cool twenty-first century, and Plaza 66 the most famous new designer shopping mall, but for most Chinese the prices at the Dior, Prada and Hermès boutiques are unaffordable. Cheaper copies are easy to come by.

◁ **Shanghai's most chic designer label shopping mall**

▽ **Street life disappears into a slick, silent, air-conditioned, plaza covering a city block topped by two commercial towers**

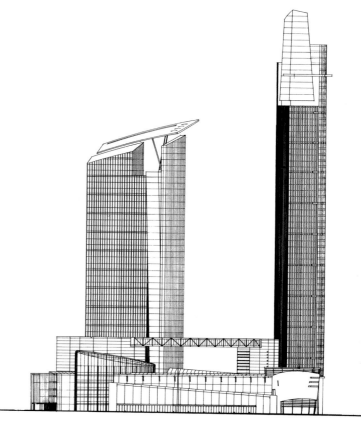

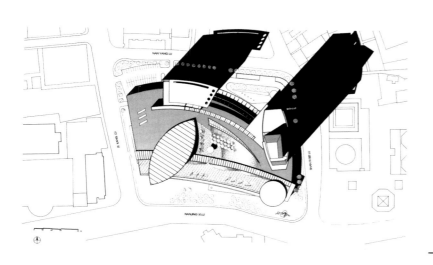

▽  Night life on Nanjing Lu

▷  A new era of Shanghai shopping

Dennis Lau & Ng Chun Man

# JINGUANGHUA RETAIL COMPLEX, RENMIN LU, SHENZHEN

Completion 2005

As a result of an international competition between six architects from Hong Kong, China, France and Japan, the architects were appointed in 2003 to construct a modern covered shopping complex as an object of urban renewal. The site lies in the middle of Shenzhen's most popular shopping avenues, Renmin Lu, in the Luhou district. The planning strategy is universal; well known department stores are placed as magnets within the malls and smaller local shops fill the spaces in between. Cinemas attract audiences who might also shop and restaurants in food courts offer another ambience in which to meet friends, who might also shop. The strategy of linking public transport and commerce is also not new but shows a further sophistication in Chinese town planning. The basement level of the arcade will have direct access to the main concourse of Renmin underground station and, hopefully, encourage shoppers to use trains rather than cars.

On a site of 17,400 square metres, a gross floor area of 80,000 square metres will be built over eight storeys and two basements. For those with heavy or awkward packages, not transportable on the underground, there are 420 car-parking spaces.

While the building type is not any different to shopping complexes in other developed countries the progress here is in the attempt to integrate temporary advertising signage in the permanent architecture. Earlier retail centres in China have proved to be particularly vulnerable to disfigurement by poorly planned billboards. Advertising, as a prerequisite of the new, market-orientated China, cannot be banned but the challenge has been for the architects to provide ample space which will not lower the building's reputation in years to come. As the buying public becomes more aware of international design standards the atmosphere in these temples of consumption has to become more calm and refined, to attract both the better educated and more affluent customers, and consequently the more up-market retail stores and chains.

The box-like façade, a steel and glass container, becomes the neutral backdrop for a four-storey high prime advertising poster space. Rented out as an advertising opportunity, and continually renewed, this is an official acknowledgement of advertising graphics as public artwork. What is the difference between this form of marketing and the 'big poster' art of Mao's era? Only the message has changed.

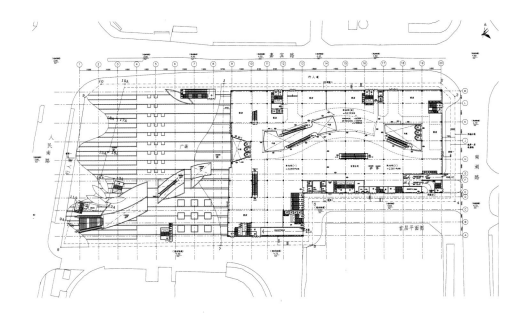

◁ A narrative layout of routes across the site

▷ top Big posters as marketing messages
bottom In the world of shopping we're all one in the global mall

gmp von Gerkan, Marg und Partner

# CONVENTION AND EXHIBITION CENTRE (SZCEC), SHENZHEN

Completed 2004

Hemmed in by a forest of first and second-generation, non-descript towers, differentiated in age by height, the SZCEC is a relatively low-lying, 280 x 540-square-metre blanket over Shenzhen's urban landscape. A rank of pin jointed, steel, portal frames form the carcass of a one-level exhibition hall, double the length of gmp's earlier 1996 Leipzig Exhibition Centre. The aerial image is similar to that of a barrow burial mound dwarfing the elements of the surrounding multi-million city. An elevated entrance, rising to an observation platform 7.50 metres above the centre of the exhibition volume, cuts through one of the long elevations and brings congress visitors to a separately articulated tube shaped conference facility, supported on sixty-metre-high, steel A-frames at intervals of thirty metres, fifteen metres above the exhibition hall spine.

This is yet another variation in the trade hall and congress facilities building type in which functional requirements, geared to commerce, display flexibility, heavy vehicle transport and visitor traffic, override considerations of human scale. The best result is to be able to achieve an impressive landmark, which becomes a unique marketing label for the location, and is seamlessly integrated with the surrounding traffic routes for air and land access which will not transform the rest of the city into one, huge, traffic grid lock.

References to Shenzhen's similarity with London's 1852 Crystal Palace are inevitable with its glass cladding, fountains and water features, combined with colourful illumination and night floodlighting. But, whereas Crystal Palace was a hand-crafted, innovative prototype, this is a pre-packed solution necessary to meet the demands of global trade and the one world market. Not everything can be bought and sold on the Internet or discussed using video conferencing. There have to be cities and locations where such giants must be accommodated, and increasingly so in China which is becoming the fulcrum of international exchange.

◁ Contrasting scales, international trade vs urban fabric

Facilities for global marketing bear analogy with a great industrial machine architecture in which human scale plays a minor role

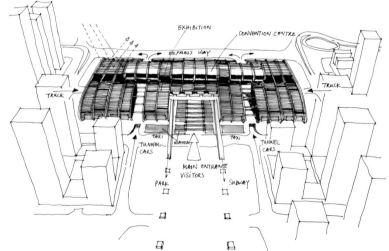

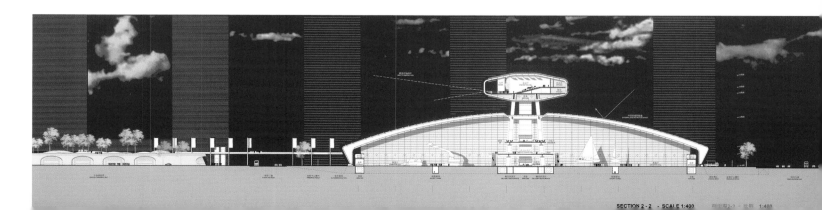

SECTION 2-2 · SCALE 1:400

# INTERNATIONAL EXPO CENTRE, SUZHOU

Completion 2005

Located in the Yangtze basin Suzhou is a rapidly expanding city with a 2,500-year-old historic city centre, partially still intact. An ancient proverb says: "In Heaven there is paradise, on earth Suzhou and Hangzhou." When the Grand Canal was completed in the Sui Dynasty (589–618) Suzhou found itself strategically placed on an important trade route. Built on commerce and especially famous for its silk industry, the city relied on man-made waterways for transport. By the twelfth century the city was criss-crossed by six north-south, and fourteen east-west, canals. Although most of these have now been filled in the city has retained a little of it's 'Renaissance' character first described for the western world by Marco Polo. In 1896 Suzhou was opened to foreign trade. Japanese and other international concessions were located in the city. Now trade is once again influencing the city's architecture, but in new ways. Suzhou's famous ancient gardens, traditional neighbourhood walled compounds, cobbled streets and low bridges are preserved as tourist attractions while the commercial and industrial functions have been banned to the city margins with sustainable water, power, drainage and rubbish recycling systems.

The Expo Centre, as part of a growing Suzhou Industrial Park Convention and Exhibition Centre, is a new phenomenon in China. Combining opportunities for local manufacturers to display their wares to foreign buyers and international standards in hotel and conference facilities, the aim is to stimulate business connections and build networks which in turn lead on to profitable exchanges. The architecture for this concept is dependent on supporting global banking, telecommunications and transport systems, already being in place.

Trade-fair architecture needs only a shed to satisfy functional requirements but here the architects have based their design on the concept of a fan. This forms the framework for future building extensions and also gives the project a unique character, transforming it into a landmark. Breaking up the building mass into a series of low, two-storey, repetitive pavilions lends human scale to what are essentially industrial-scale halls, and protects the visitor from being too overwhelmed by the dimensions of a global marketplace. The column-free, upper level sub-halls are configured to provide a continuous exhibition space of more than 70,000 square metres and, as such, is one of the largest open exhibition spaces in the world.

Unfolding across the site, the total accommodation with a floor area of 320,000 square metres is constructed of local materials, using standard structural solutions in steel and concrete, glass and green granite. At the heart of the plan is a public park for relaxation between business deals and for contemplation on how to clinch the next one. Pools, lined by gardens, connect the existing canals which flank the site and tie the complex into the Suzhou Industrial Park.

▽  **Site planning based on the fan principle for easy extension**

▷ **top  The unfolding Chinese fan principle**
**bottom  Focus is centred on a water front with gardens**

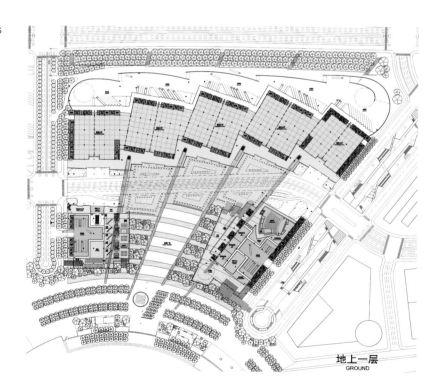

地上一层
GROUND

five

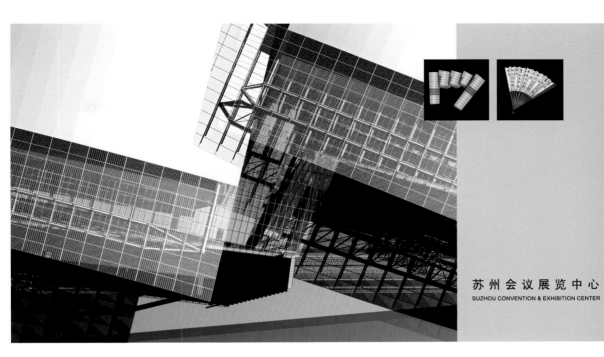

苏州会议展览中心
SUZHOU CONVENTION & EXHIBITION CENTER

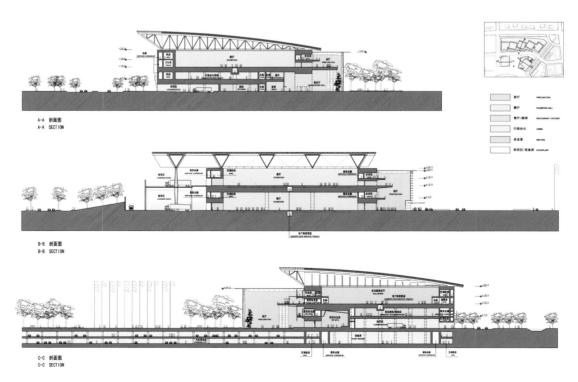

A—A 剖面图
A—A SECTION

B—B 剖面图
B—B SECTION

C—C 剖面图
C—C SECTION

◁ top  Light, low and spacious forecourts

▽ Roofed but glazed plazas make use of natural light while protecting be-suited visitors from climate extremes

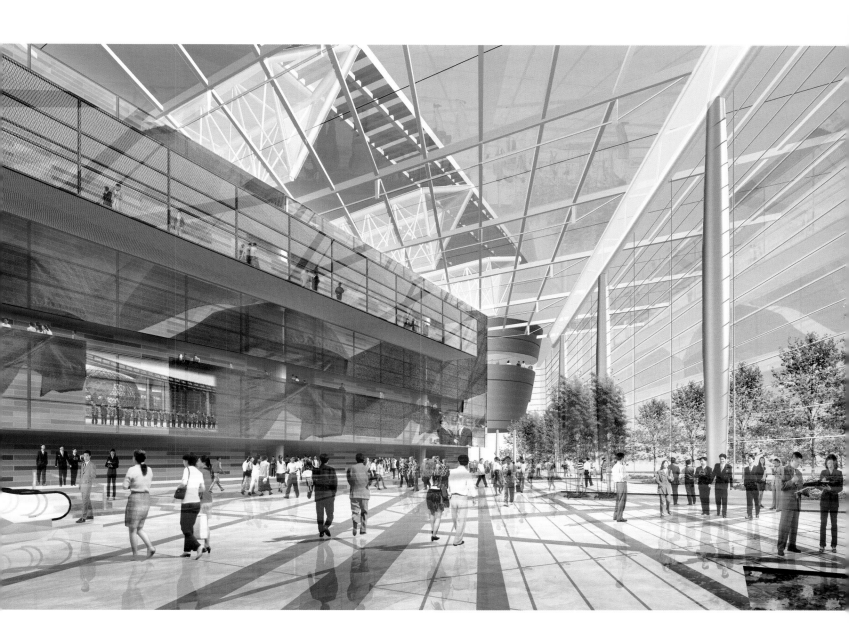

# INTERNATIONAL AUTOMOTIVE EXPO, BEIJING

Completion 2007

The People's Republic of China has decided to make automobile production and science one of the country's major industries. From an economy which previously emphasized agriculture and the traditional heavy industries this very much reflects the move into a consumer-orientated society. Whether this is reasonable in a world of diminishing raw materials and increasing pollution is debatable but, maybe, this concentration on mobility technology will lead to the development and use of sustainable fuels and recycling processes which will assuage our guilt.

This eighty-five-hectare oblong site, located in the south-west of the metropole on the 4th Ring road, is planned as a permanent international motor show, with past, present, and future models from the world's car brands. The architects, who previously designed Volkswagen's Auto City in Wolfsburg, Germany, as a family attraction with publicity and sales centres in a collection of museums in a park, has been given an even broader canvass on which to play. As one of sixty mega-projects for visitors to the Beijing Olympics the construction has to be complete before 2008.

The design is said to have been conceived as a contemporary, open, and no longer forbidden, Imperial City. Symbolic of the overthrow of the Old Order, and as a pointer to China's new technological thrust into the twenty-first century, the project is weighed down with expectations which can only be satisfied by spectacular architecture and sensory effects. At the centre of the park the history, present and future, of automobile development is to be played out in a theatrical 'Middle Kingdom'. Continual visual references are made between a glorious past and a glorious future. The car pavilions are described as 'glass rocks in the park', a reference to the Chinese garden art of displaying water eroded rocks as sculptures.

From the main entrance visitors will be drawn into a spectacular 40,000-square-metre automobile museum in the shape of a giant teardrop on many sweeping levels, through the length of the site, past the many other attractions to end up facing a new university devoted to the automobile sciences, technology and marketing. On either side of this central route, with bridges over a lake and artificial islands, symmetrical blocks of service buildings for brand name motor companies will provide 151,000 square metres for their vehicle markets and sales pavilions, and 35,000 square metres for vehicle examination workshops, mixed in with 50,000 square metres of shopping malls and 85,000 square metres for an hotel and congress centre. Administration offices of 140,000 square metres, with underground car parking for 5,600 vehicles, complete this car-city. Heavily planted and landscaped, the 120,000-square-metre park with water features aims to contrast with the man made world of machines.

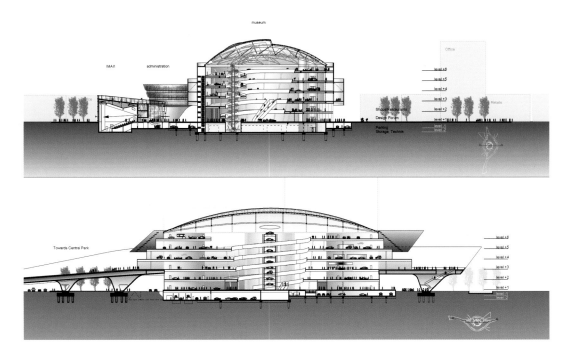

◁ **Sections through the changing volumes of the automobile museum**

▷ **The teardrop shaped museum is the centre piece of an eighty-five hectare park landscape dedicated to the freedom of movement on four wheels**

◁ Architecture as frozen, dynamic, music in swirls and curves giving the illusion
of speed while stationary

△ The museum interior as wheels within wheels

Kohn Pedersen Fox Associates

# ZHONGGUANCUN WEST, BSTP LOT 21, HAIDIAN, BEIJING

Under construction

Constructed for the Beijing Science and Technology Park this thirty-five-storey concrete, steel and glass sheathed, multi-purpose project with a technology, exhibition and conference centre, offices and associated residential, hotel and retail, units, is planned as a national icon representing the importance of the sciences in China's future. It was chosen as one of the finalists in the 2003 Beijing Architecture Awards.

The Tsing Hua master plan established Lot 21 as a sweeping arc, expressed in a bridge building, housing the exhibition hall and restaurant which links a tower to the north and a podium to the south. This construction frames the views of the two adjacent parks, connects the two office blocks and also acts as gateway to the centre of the site. The axis running through this arc-gateway marks the historical route taken by the Ming Dowager Empress when she travelled from her court in the Forbidden City to her Summer Palace in the north-west of Beijing. Few people standing in front of the completed building will know this historical detail. The fact that the architect feels required to give the design some anchor in the nation's past says a lot about the way Chinese clients want to see their development as the continuum of a glorious, even if feudal and terrible, past.

The public, in whichever country, always expects the appearance of an advanced science establishment to be something space-age and alien to everyday architecture. To convey the idea of an energetic, futuristic, enterprise the architectural forms here are curved planes and volumes clad in glass and metal. Instead of boxes, cylinders or spheres, the imagery tries to break out of conventional building order and is described by the architect as unfolding, like petals or feathers. Perhaps the analogy of a space module landing on the moon would be more appropriate. From a distance the vertical fins on the external walls will add texture which will shimmer and glint depending on the angle of view. In keeping with progressive sciences it exhibits the buildings technical services specifications are said to be of the highest standards, as yet, to be found in the Chinese capital.

◁ Sloping ceilings put a new slant on windowless circulation spaces

△ A bridge structure, containing exhibition hall and restaurant, linking the north tower
and southern podium looks like a landed fish

Terrestrial and heavenly bodies, planets spinning in their orbits, all brought together around a traditionally planned, Chinese walled garden

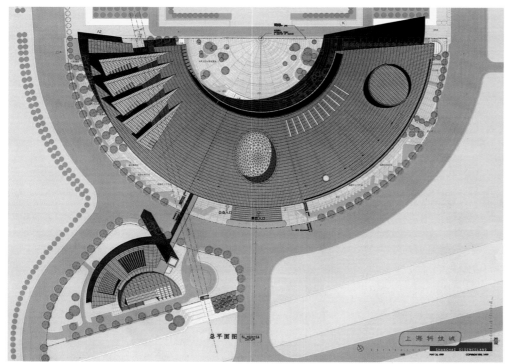

RTKL Associates

# MUSEUM OF SCIENCE AND TECHNOLOGY, PUDONG, SHANGHAI

Completed 2001

This 89,000 square metre science museum is designed as an educational instrument to promote interest in new technology. Many school parties visit the museum with their teachers and many exhibits have a high entertainment component to encourage or awake curiosity. The complex of two structures sits on the Southside of Pudong Civic Plaza, opposite the New Area Government Building and next to Pudong Central Park. Century Avenue, and a new subway line, make the centre very accessible for private and public transport and, until the opening of the Oriental Art Centre, it is the biggest public attraction in an otherwise sterile piece of city planning. In contrast to the empty streets outside the Museum is always full and rings with the chatter and laughter of children and family groups.

The four storey main block houses five galleries on the themes universe, living, intelligence, innovation, and future. In a central glazed hall lined with interactive screens, connecting two gallery wings and a research library with administrative and service areas, a "floating" spherical cinema "hangs" between walkways from the higher levels. The aesthetic idea is to rep-

resent an incubator for scientific advance, a yoke developing within an egg. Virtually all Chinese modern architecture quotes the harmony between Man and Nature, as reflected in the use of all five elements, metal, wood, fire, water and earth, comprising building and surroundings. It would, in fact, be difficult to build a building without using all these elements but the formula has become de rigueur in the description of any project presentation.

All the theatrical stops have been pulled out to give visitors the feeling of circulating within a vortex of swirling movement, the primordial soup of the nascent universe. Raked elevations and walls increase the feeling of soaring height. A dynamic spiral form, executed in translucent and reflective glass, and a monolithic flying roof, is intended to symbolize the gathering pace of China's economic and scientific advance, and Man's continuing search for answers beyond the stars. The grand sweeping curved façade, which both overlooks and embraces the Civic Plaza, is almost entirely transparent, inviting the public to enter.

Inside and outside are fluid concepts but despite gigantic heights and immense open spaces the architecture fails to intimidate the museum's chief users, school parties and family groups.

Dennis Lau & Ng Chun Man

# HUA WEI TECHNOLOGIES HEADQUARTERS AND INTERNATIONAL TRAINING CENTRE, BUJI BANTIAN, LONG GANG DISTRICT, SHENZHEN

Training Centre completed 2002; Headquarters Building completed 2004

Established in 1988 Hua Wei Technologies employ 15,000 staff in over thirty countries. Their factory, international training centre and offices at Buji Bantian are set in a park landscape which is well-used by staff and visitors. This semi-rural concept for large companies started in developed countries with the English garden cities and in the US with corporation headquarters in the 1950s. That this form is now being used in mainland China is an indication of the countries developing maturity. Earlier, and still existing, Special Economic Zone sweatshop factories set down in the middle of dustbowls can only survive so long as people are desperate for jobs and no better conditions are available. International companies today must also care for their international images.

The first stage International Training Centre is a low-rise, two to three-storey complex of six blocks. Architecturally it is restrained and functional with the appearance of a college campus. Materials and forms are generic to the region and wet sub-tropical climate. Deeply recessed windows keep the sun at bay and pitched roofs throw off torrential rains. Construction labour and materials, earth toned ceramics, block-work, grey interlocking roof tiles, Shantou natural granites and rusticated stone finishes, were all locally sourced. The overall impression is of permanence and solidity, and at the same time there is variety of layout, levels and landscaping. A circulation spine for the complex runs through the teaching pavilions, then spreads out to three satellite conference pavilions and a catering and restaurant area able to serve the many nationalities of visitors, staff and students. The aim of the architecture is to make the environment conducive to large gatherings, small meetings and casual interaction between people. Generous corridors, alcoves and bay windows within the buildings are matched by a variety of differently organized and planted areas, including a cloister garden of 2,500 square metres in the surrounding park.

The second development within the same company park is the administrative headquarters. Again, the concept is quality understatement in the interests of a tranquil working atmosphere. There are single offices, suites of offices and meeting rooms for top level management. Two main groups of buildings are located at either end of an ornamental lake. A larger accounts and marketing wing comprises a cluster of pavilions, each on a nine-by-twelve-metre, structural grid and between 1,500 to 2,500 square metres in area, connected to each other by lift lobbies so that expansion can be accommodated either horizontally or vertically. At the centre of each pavilion is a full height landscaped open air courtyard so that natural light reaches into all levels. The separate VIP wing, served by an independent entrance, is another self contained cluster of offices, meeting rooms, restaurant and support facilities with more private offices overlooking a second ornamental lake.

Hua Wei Technologies have understood the difference between the form and substance of hi-tech architecture. A traditional looking, unspectacular, appearance gives little clue to the more sophisticated building techniques and planning involved, from high level insulation to life cycle costing, reduced energy and maintenance issues, and materials and building systems chosen for their long life and adaptability qualities.

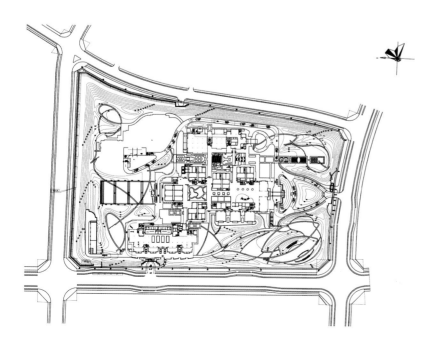

Like a model English Garden Suburb, business park or college campus, the architecture gives no clue as to the epoch making research and developments which are taking place behind these staid and tranquil facades. High priority has been given to the creation of a peaceful environment in which the mind is free to explore a cyber world.

MADA s.p.a.m.

# ZHEJIANG UNIVERSITY LIBRARY, NINGBO CAMPUS, ZHEJIANG

Completed 2002

Ningbo Campus is a student city of ten tertiary educational institutions and university faculties grouped together outside Ningbo city centre. The architects were commissioned by all the different institutions to design their individual buildings but the 29,900-square-metre library, over nine levels, is the highest structure and a focus for the whole campus. It occupies a hinge position between living and teaching quarters, and between the campus park running east-west, and the major, internal, north-south circulation axis. The building has no 'front' or 'back'. The library block's four façades have been given equal weighting and importance with interlocking panels of purple-red tiling and set-backs of raw-looking, timber planking.

Internally the library's form was inspired by the ancient Chinese Scripture Pavilion, *cang-jing-ge*, a room for the storage of sacred books within a temple. Book learning and scholars have always been highly revered in Chinese culture and Ningbo is the site of China's oldest surviving library. The Tianyige Library, built in 1516, was founded by Fan Qin, a Ming official, for his collection of books, local history documentation (including lists of the successful candidates in Imperial examinations), wood-blocks, and handwritten copies of Confucian classics which go back to the eleventh century.

Seclusion and contemplation were the architect's reasons for wrapping the library into the confines of a protective citadel structure. Book stacks are arranged around the outside walls of the library. Carved out of this thick, insulating, perimeter pro-

tection of books, more private reading nooks have been created which are then articulated on the building's exterior. The large, central void is inhabited by 'floating spaces', used for an Internet café, reading lounge, cataloguing and group functions. Books, which are stable and permanent, enclose the readers, who are ephemeral and in constant flux. The architect's spatial interpretation of an historical Chinese Scripture Pavilion means that the books create a centre but do not occupy it.

The rest of the campus consists of a sports stadium, lecture rooms, administration and residential blocks. These all have their own individual faces within various size blocks with flat or asymmetrically sloping roofs and grid-organized elevations of reinforced concrete, brick and coloured panels. The hard landscaping is chessboard-chequered and contains only a few isolated, singular trees as centrepieces to formal squares framed by low walling which additionally serves as seating. Formal organizational techniques contrast with informal layouts. Squares beside odd-shaped, angular courtyards, all funnelled towards the library site, set up interesting visual tensions.

The architect admits that the speed of construction—the campus was completed in a year—did not allow for the growth of the environment in reaction to use. Despite this disadvantage the campus exhibits none of the dead atmosphere of many other artificially created establishments. The campus, as a whole, is a good example of what Qingyun Ma describes as 'conceptional urbanism' in which different uses are brought together in a collage.

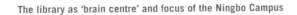

**The library as 'brain centre' and focus of the Ningbo Campus**

gmp von Gerkan, Marg und Partner

# GERMAN SCHOOL AND APARTMENTS, BEIJING

Completed 2000

Embassies and expatriate institutions in foreign countries occupy a special architectural category. Their architects are usually chosen from home and their clients are, first and foremost, their own nationals who feel most comfortable in an architectural style they recognize. On the other hand national pride and foreign policy dictate that the edifices should be representative, exemplary, and display all the good and marketable aspects of their nation, many thousands of miles away and in another climate zone, which they would dearly like their host to buy into.

The architectural competition for a German school and employee's apartments was held shortly before Germany's political reunification in 1998. The wedge shaped compound on a major traffic intersection, accommodating both the 9,658 square metre school and the separate 9,657 square metre block containing forty-five apartments, has very little to do with the surrounding developments flanking the Liangmaqiao Lu in the Third Embassy District. This multi-lane arterial road to the north-east of Beijing is the main route to and from the capital's airport. In late 2004 neighbouring structures were a dilapidated looking restaurant and bar called Schiller's, recently completed expensive private apartments in landscaping behind a high wrought iron fence, a fortified and security patrolled Israeli embassy and, on the opposite side of the road, a luxury Kempinski Hotel and shabby Lufthansa first generation shopping centre with plastic beer garden. Nearby large tracts had been levelled and were awaiting new construction while contractors seemed to have lost interest in a half-completed

and abandoned commercial block languishing behind chained gates.

In contrast the German compound, with two or three-storey, horizontal school wings, connected to a hub of foyer, sports areas and great hall, alongside a more vertical residential complex of two parallel, nine-storey blocks, is an inviting development, combining human scale, trees, planting, and warm colour combinations. The original welcoming concept has unfortunately been undermined by subsequent security measures; a second garrison-fence beyond the perimeter strip of street landscaping, inspection procedures and controlled access with heavy weight guards.

The apartments are clad in Italian yellow panels with emphasized joint lines forming a grid across the elevations. A system of full height concertina folding louvered window shutters enforces the Mediterranean look. Corner windows allow panoramic views to the neighbourhood and break the rigid block lines. On the flat roof solar panels have been added since construction. The school blocks are clad in Umbrian red panels with a similar delineation of joint lines and vertical narrow window fenestration. Both constructions have exposed dark grey 'flying buttress' steel beams and columns further emphasising the controlling three dimensional grid order.

As in historical Chinese compounds everything behind the walls is exclusive and concealed. Passersby do not profit from glimpses of the lawns, avenues of trees, views of sports courts or sculpture hidden between the building wings.

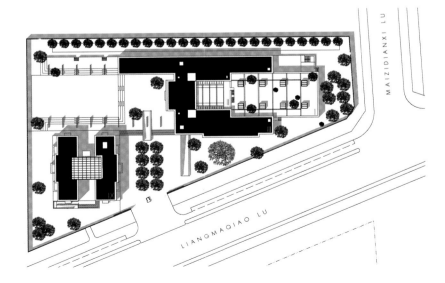

◁ A triangular site in the newer embassy district on the way to Beijing Capital Airport

△ Staff apartments, separate but within the school compound

▽ Sliding window louvre detail

△  Hard and soft landscaping with shaded areas for sitting outside

▷  A strong grid framework for inset windows, shutters,
colonnades and quirky sculptures

Rocco Design

# GUANGZHOU LIBRARY, ZHUJIANG NEW TOWN, GUANGZHOU'S NEW CITY CENTRE

Competition won 2005; completion 2007

This is another of the 'special objects' which will form a group of cultural palaces at the heart of Guangzhou's new Pearl River waterfront. It will stand opposite Zaha Hadid's Opera House and a Children's Activity Centre, and beside the Quangdong Museum which Rocco Yim won in earlier international competition.

Libraries are universal architectural types. They need to satisfy two building users; inanimate books, which need care if they are not to disintegrate, and people who want to study individually, meet in groups and perhaps also be entertained. None of these functions are specifically 'Chinese' but the architect has tried to symbolically marry the design with its location and users with images based on three-dimensional Chinese puzzles and sinuous, free-flowing calligraphy brush strokes. Enclosed storage for books interlocks with the light and airy,

modulated and landscaped areas for people. The puzzle is an allegory for intellectual exploration and, although they are opposite in character, the two blocks interlock, mediating across an internal street volume. The balance between being extroverted and introverted, between daylight and shadow, between enclosed and transparent spaces, plays on the Ying Yang ideology although the materials and form are totally contemporary.

Few architects get the chance to design neighbouring buildings. In the current Chinese building culture of disparate 'objects' Rocco Yim has managed to employ a similar genetic code, of scale, form and geometry, for both his museum and library structures while projecting two very different characters. The museum is precious and protecting of its treasures; the library opens out and invites the public to read, learn and exchange ideas.

◁ **Light and airy public spaces**

▷ **Bird's eye view of 'Chinese puzzle'**

◁ Daylight for reading rooms

△ Internal street

Paul Andreu

# NATIONAL THEATRE, CHANG AN AVENUE, BEIJING

Completion 2005

This has been arguably China's most controversial modern design. Paul Andreu won the competition against sixty-eight other internationally known architects. The project title is modest and hides the fact that this is a complex of three auditoriums; a 2,416-seat opera house, a 2,017-seat concert hall and a 1,040-seat theatre. In between these three enormous volumes the foyer space, which will be open to the public, has an urban atmosphere with footways, bridges, balconies, squares, commercial and restaurant zones. All these functions are housed under a titanium shell roof, set down in an artificial lake, in the heart of Beijing, behind the Great Hall of the People and 500 metres from Tiananmen Square.

As the treasure house of China's most important cultural institutions, with opera the most popular national entertainment at its centre, the architecture could not have been more distinctive. The silvery titanium dome, 213 metres by 144 metres in plan, and forty-six metres high above the water level, is covered in gilt metal mesh and split through the centre by a 100 metre section of glazing. Entry is through a sixty-metre long transparent tube which burrows under the lake and emerges in the foyer at the base of the dome. Paul Andreu described the experience of entry into the complex as one of sensory contrasts, a journey through successive envelopes, a passage through experiences of light and dark, public views and concentrated private visions, with changing daylight hues filtering through the dome during the course of the day and coloured illuminations internally at night. Visitors leave everyday reality when they dive into the entrance tunnel below the water line and enter a fantastical dream world before they have set foot in any one of the performance halls.

Externally the glittering dome, an autark and mysterious alien structure, appears to float on the water without any visible connection to the lakeshore. It was perhaps not surprising that opinions were polarised. Discussions carried out in the Chinese media, at home and abroad, became a public forum for the airing of views on national identity, tradition versus modernism, and the overwhelming influence of foreign design on China's emerging representative buildings. In China it was called a 'sparkling drop of water', an 'eggshell' or a 'big tomb'. At the ninth National People's Congress in 2002 some delegates thought it was "not necessary for a developing country to build a theatre costing four times more than New York's Lincoln Center for the Performing Arts." In December 1999 *The Architectural Review* in London called it a "bombastic blob," "a familiar building type—the

airport departure lounge" with "no sense of direction, orientation or place;" the architect's previous experience on fifty international airports was seen to have inappropriately influenced his theatre design. But, although the materials and form are products of technology and modern aesthetics the move through 'gates', over or under water, bridges and enclosed airy volumes, are not foreign to Chinese classical thought on the progression between spaces.

As with all vast projects costs have increased during construction. When approved by the State Council in April 1998 the estimate was for 2.7 billion Yuan and completion was planned for 2003. After a lengthy postponement, due to doubts and criticism, construction on the 150,000 square metre site started in 2000 after fifteen months of design modifications. Completion will now be in 2005 and costs will have been trimmed back to nearly the original estimate.

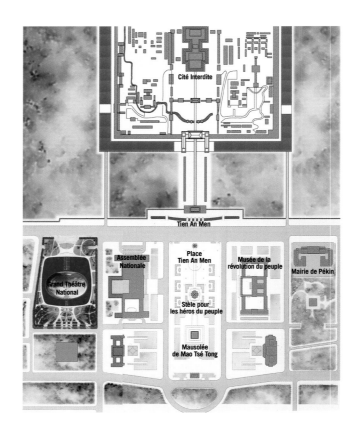

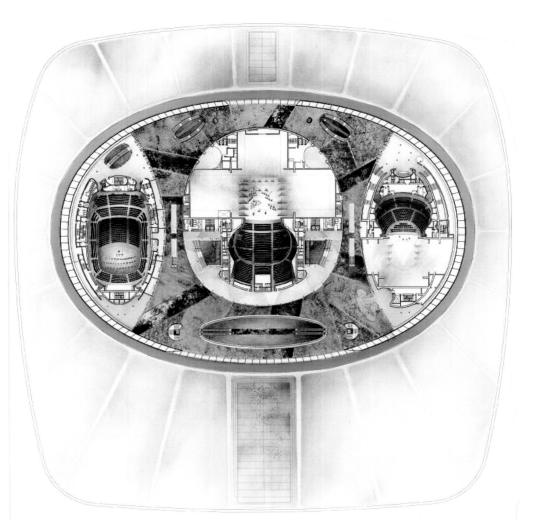

▷ The National Theatre is three
auditoriums under one shell in the
centre of a lake

▽ One of the most controversial
building projects in modern day China,
the National Theatre is decisively
different in form and materials from the
surrounding state architecture.

◁ The foyer space between the three theatres – a public forum in which to see and be seen

▽ As befitting a building of national and cultural symbolism, concerts, plays and opera, have been promised the most up-to-date facilities

Paul Andreu

# ORIENTAL ART CENTRE, CENTURY AVENUE, PUDONG, SHANGHAI

Completion 2005

Taking the form of a cluster of five differently sized cut-glass bowls the Oriental Art Centre is not easy to miss at the end of Century Avenue. It is symmetrically placed opposite RTKL's very popular Technology and Science Museum, and the Town Hall, across an expanse of multi-lane carriageway, bordered by immaculate grass verges and flower beds, which are common features of China's new civic pride.

In contrast to the many different but identical towers on the same skyline the glass bowl image is at least unique. Despite its misleading name this is a music centre of 39,694 square metres containing a 1,979-seat Philharmonic Hall, 1,054-seat Lyric Theatre, and 330-seat Chamber Music Hall with backstage areas, dressing rooms and rehearsal rooms. Slotted in between these major functions are also an arts library and multimedia training facility.

The simple external form makes the complex look smaller than it really is. There are seven levels inside all radiating from an open plan core, a common circulation and meeting area for public, performers and VIPs. Individual character is given to the three principal halls by using different colours and materials. While internally the halls are clad in enamelled ceramic the external umbrella structure has a glass coat over a perforated metal sheet. At night the effect is of lanterns in the mist and the tapered base of the bowls makes the structure look concentrated and rooted on site.

The project's cultural intention is to found a centre of artistic excellence which will bring together in lively meetings public and musicians from very varied backgrounds. Acoustics in the halls are designed to cater for modern or ancient compositions, including western and Chinese opera. Marooned at the end of Century Avenue it seems a very small cultural drop, without a supportive background, in the ocean of Pudong's relentless commercial activity.

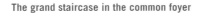

**The grand staircase in the common foyer**

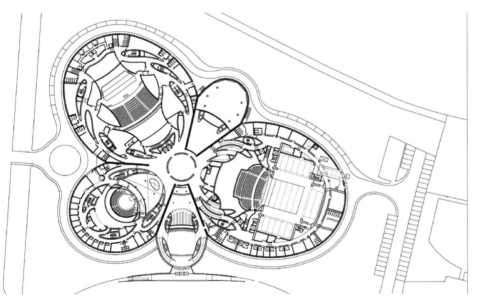

△ The glass bowls at night
◁ A cluster plan of five, interrelated music venues
▽ Interiors with Art Deco lines

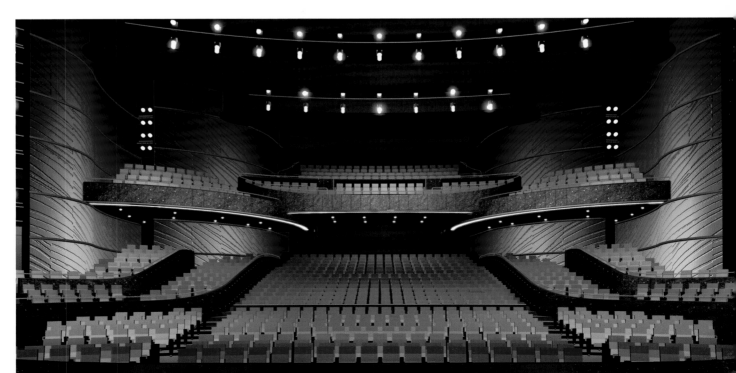

# GUANGZHOU OPERA HOUSE, GUANGZHOU, GUANGDONG PROVINCE

Completion 2007

Given the status of Guangzhou as a great bustling city and opera as an almost sacred national artistic entertainment, the proposed new Opera House is envisioned as an opulent institution with a 1,800-seat Grand Theatre, multifunctional hall, suitably grandiose entrance lobbies and lounges. State-of-the-art back stage technology and supporting facilities are planned to ensure this cultural institution can take its place among the worlds finest. Total floor area will be 46,000 square metres.

Design drawings show an amorphous architecture of dynamic and generous, flowing, volumes which the architect describes as two rock formations. It is hard to imagine them as static pieces of architecture fixed on the ground. Lines are more curvaceous than earlier works and hopefully the final built forms will not stray too far from this original design. It will be interesting to see the chosen construction materials.

Located down stream from the Pearl River the proposed twin boulders silhouette of contoured landmasses is intended to mediate between metropolitan centre, a future museum quarter and the riverside and dock area. Located on Zhujiang Boulevard the site is near the Haixinsha Tourist Park Island. When seen from the boulevard the Opera House complex should appear as a visual introduction to the island. To strengthen the connection to related cultural centres an internal street is planned to cut through the Opera House boulders to meet up with the proposed new museums on the opposite side of Zhujiang Boulevard. The setting will be dramatic against a backdrop of skyscrapers in the Zhujiang New Town, the river, and docks across the water.

No cultural experience is complete without a good bar, restaurant and shopping opportunities. These services are to be embedded into the base of the 'land forms' beside the promenade approach to the Opera House. Visitors cars and buses have a drop-off point on the north side from Huajiu Road while service vehicles can enter from either end of the same road, and very important visitors are to have a reserved entrance on the western boundary off Huaxia Road.

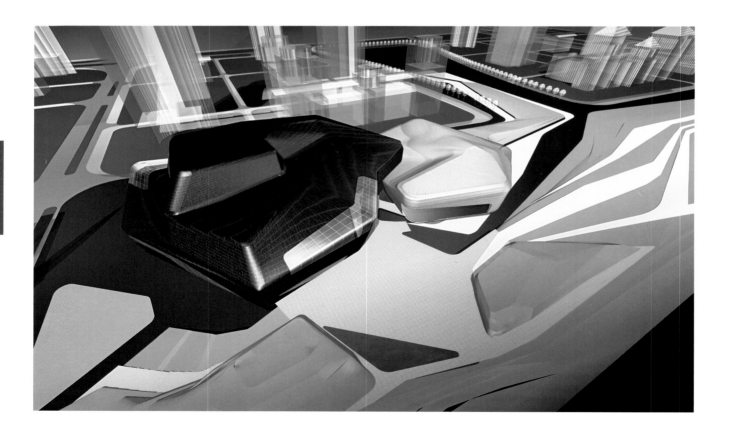

◁ Land forms looking like
no other known buildings

△ Low lying boulders in the
urban landscape

▽ An opera auditorium, hopefully,
as dramatic as this architect's
drawing

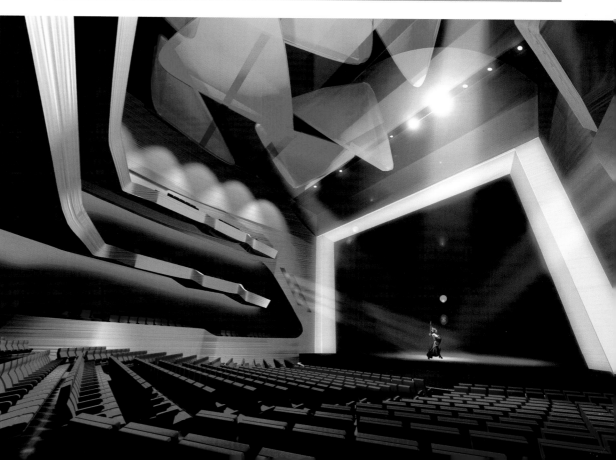

# SUZHOU ART MUSEUM, SUZHOU

In planning

The new Suzhou Art Museum is planned for the northeast section of the historic quarter of Suzhou, beside the Garden of the Humble Administrator, a sixteenth-century garden which is listed as a UNESCO World Heritage site. Suzhou is only a couple of hours by train from Shanghai and a very popular tourist destination. The city which is endeavouring to maintain its historical structure and buildings while modernizing its public services and creating new trade and industrial centres is clogged in the tourist season with buses and sight seeing groups who wander from one historic garden to the next by way of the narrow cobbled lanes. The existing Suzhou Museum is housed in an historic house planned around several open courtyards and gardens which originally belonged to a highly decorated general, Zhong Wang of the Taiping Heavenly Kingdom.

The planned art museum will make reference to the traditional vocabulary of white-washed plaster, dark grey, clay roof tiles, tree-lined avenues and private gardens which were designed as intellectual and artistic exercises for contemplation, away from court or traders intrigues, but reinterpret these ingredients in a contemporary way. In total 15,000 square metres of floor space will include 7,000 square metres for display, a 200 seat auditorium, library and storage area with curators workshops and offices. As in all their work, from Hong Kong to Beijing, the architects have tried to develop a direction for modern Chinese architecture. Their designs could be summed up as restrained good taste executed in a reduced number of quality materials.

Taking the form of the traditional courtyard building the museum will be organized around gardens and enclosed spaces which mediate between contrasting environments. The main Museum Garden is to be a commentary on the adjacent Garden of the Humble Administrator to the north. In Chinese called Zhuozheng, this ancient garden has many water features, bridges, and islands of bamboo, covering five hectares of land which is subdivided into east, middle and west sections, each with their different painterly characteristics. Although there is no visual connection between the old and new gardens, because of the high perimeter walls, water is to be used physically and metaphorically as a bridge over the intervening centuries and the two properties. The smaller Gallery Gardens and Administrative Gardens will also respect the ancient garden vocabulary but be modern in character.

As early as the eleventh century Suzhou was an intellectually cultivated city with 359 canal bridge, twelve pagodas and more than fifty temples. At the peak of Suzhou's development in the sixteenth century there were over one hundred gardens. When Marco Polo arrived in 1276 he was astonished at the large number of craftspeople, rich merchants, sages, doctors and magicians. Previously famous as a retreat for aristocracy, respected scholars, actors and artists, by 1988 the population had grown to 600,000 and around 500 new business enterprises had sprung up following the Open Door policy. Perhaps the Art Museum will go some way to restoring the balance between historical and modern China.

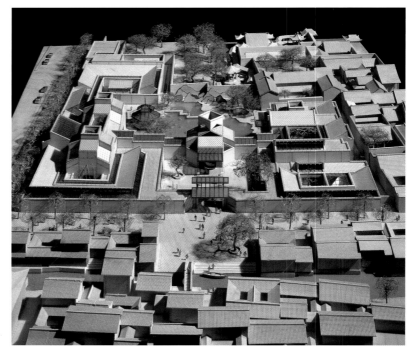

Set in the Wedgwood Willow Pattern city of Suzhou the museum maintains a low, residential atmosphere of private and public courtyard gardens and pavilions

# GUANGDONG MUSEUM, ZHUJIANG NEW TOWN, GUANGZHOU'S NEW CITY CENTRE

Competition won 2004

For a Hong Kong Chinese architect to win the Guangdong Museum against an invited list of international star architects was an outstanding achievement. Rocco Yim conceived the pristine cube floating above a podium as a monumental *object d' or* in which to keep and display treasures. In his design description he used the allegory of a sculptured antique box or lacquered jewellery case. The aim of the architecture is to raise the image of the museum to that of a cultural icon and with this in mind the park landscape flows under the body of the museum to set it off visually against the back-drop of river, belts of trees and the city skyline.

Internally the functions are organized in concentric layers, like an ivory carving of intricately fashioned, and independent, volumes within volumes. Moving inwards first come the exhibition areas with both cellular galleries and open loft spaces for larger art works. A circulation path, called a spine, weaves its way through these spaces. Punctuating the galleries are break-out alcoves, cosy and intimate in contrast to the exhibition rooms and filled with diffuse natural lighting, to give visitors resting areas with windows to the city outside. The service zone forms a loop, joining up with all the public areas, in order to be able to provide flexible back-up in various combinations. An atrium ring is a distinct route, linking all four halls and activity centres, such as audiovisual facilities, museum shop and library, which is useful for visitors to orientate themselves within the complex. A central hall doubles as the museum's main entrance and at the core an open air patio reintroduces the natural world into the Man made architecture.

Rocco Yim has always maintained that in the geometry and hierarchy of volumes, and the contrast between internal and external spaces, there can be a Chinese modern architectural vocabulary. This, his most prominent building outside Hong Kong to date, gives him a platform on which to prove his theory.

The museum is one of the provincial 'special objects', along with Zaha Hadid's Opera House, placed around the Cultural and Art Square which has been positioned on the main axis of the city, near the Pearl River

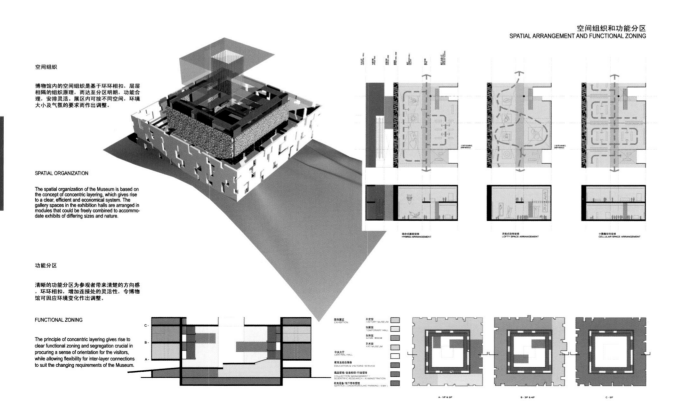

空间组织和功能分区
SPATIAL ARRANGEMENT AND FUNCTIONAL ZONING

空间组织

博物馆内的空间组织是基于环环相扣，层层相隔的组织原理，而达至分区明朗，功能合理，安排灵活。展区内可按不同空间，环境大小及气氛的要求而作出调整。

SPATIAL ORGANIZATION

The spatial organization of the Museum is based on the concept of concentric layering, which gives rise to a clear, efficient and economical system. The gallery spaces in the exhibition halls are arranged in modules that could be freely combined to accommodate exhibits of differing sizes and nature.

功能分区

清晰的功能分区为参观者带来清楚的方向感，环环相扣，增加连接处的灵活性，令博物馆可因应环境变化作出调整。

FUNCTIONAL ZONING

The principle of concentric layering gives rise to clear functional zoning and segregation crucial in procuring a sense of orientation for the visitors, while allowing flexibility for inter-layer connections to suit the changing requirements of the Museum.

博物馆透视图 View of Museum

△ The museum as jewel box set on a small hill

▽ The jewellery box on the right with Zaha Hadid's land forms opposite

△ The open air patio at the core
Halls with diffuse natural light
▽ Concentric layers

▷ A central hall foyer as plaza
with water and daylight

seven

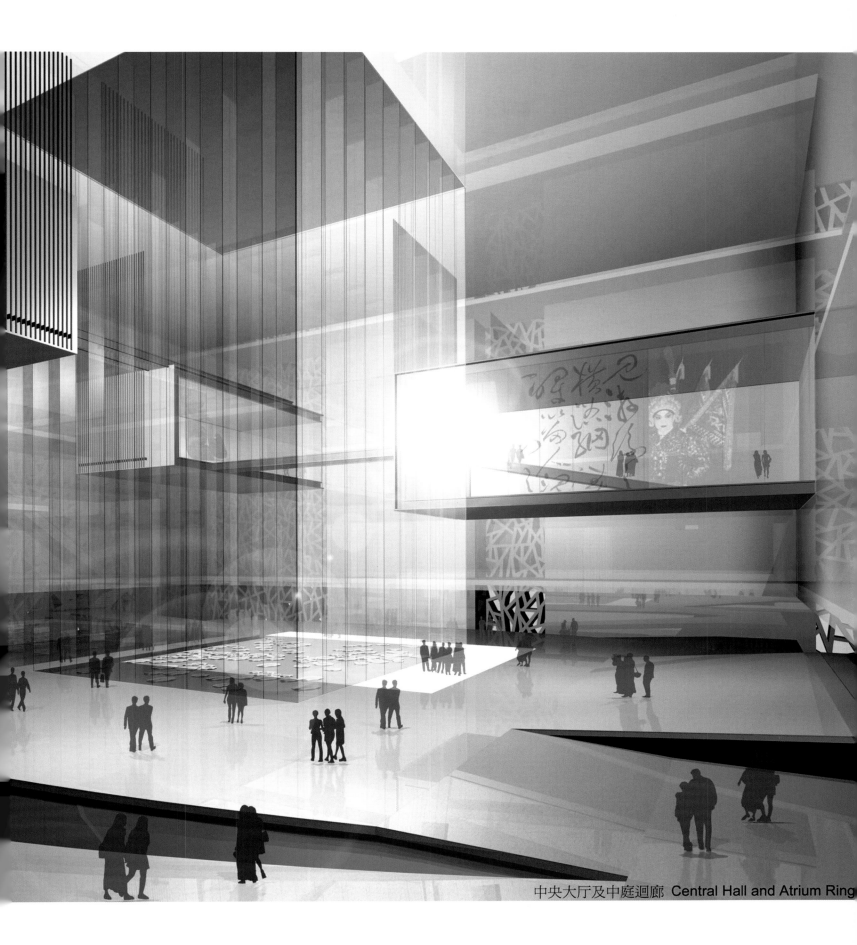

中央大厅及中庭迴廊 Central Hall and Atrium Ring

RTKL Associates

# CHINESE MUSEUM OF FILM, BEIJING

Opening 2005 to commemorate a century of Chinese cinema

The Museum of Film is another of the many non-sport projects planned for completion before the Olympics as part of the cultural get-to-know-China programme. Within a total area of 34,500 square metres there are four exhibition levels of 19,000 square metres showing film history, technology and temporary displays, a 6,000-square-metre cinema complex with IMAX theatre, a 400-seat theatre, three smaller review halls and a multifunctional hall, storage area for collections cover 2,400 square metres and research and administration functions occupy over 6,200 square metres. The project is a composition of glass, steel and black, perforated steel mesh panels, with interwoven green climbing plants and functional areas coded with coloured lights.

The People's Republic is determined to display all the best aspects of Chinese culture, with an emphasis on both traditional and modern arts and technologies. China's film industry evolved dramatically over the last half of the twentieth century and today some of the most thought provoking and sumptuously staged films are of Chinese origin with political, contemporary and historical themes.

This unique national museum will be located in a newly planned entertainment district near Beijing's airport. Without an immediate urban setting the museum is designed to have a self-sustained integrity. As a themed experience for a wide international audience the architecture has made use of Pop Art visuals and film techniques which need few words of explanation to be impressive. Taking its cue from a universal film icon, the production clapboard, giant translucent glass walls covered in projected images are angled toward the main public entrance, while the museum itself is a simple black rectangular box. Visitors progressing from one staged event to another are hardly aware of the actual architecture. Solid reality remains outside and the impression is created of a journey through a dematerialised world.

Internally the layout for exhibits is based on spatial planning tricks used in classical Chinese gardens where the choreographed labyrinth of vistas over a long distance are interwoven with smaller spaces tucked away for improvisational viewings. As in the film world of celluloid the architecture blurs the boundaries between real and virtual, fantasy and documentary, human and heroic scale. The aim is to present both a factual archive and an entertaining emotional experience.

seven

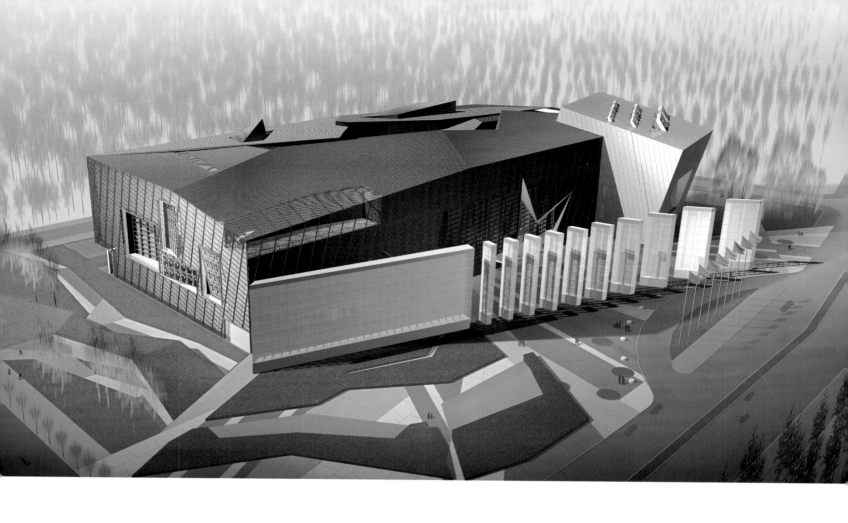

The Film Museum is all about illusory spaces and ephemeral images rather than concrete architecture

RTKL

中国电影博物馆 CHINESE MUSEUM OF FILM

RTKL

中国电影博物馆 Chinese Museum of Film

From the outside to the inside the museum consists of a sequence of experiences in which real space plays only a functional role or provides a theatrical setting, as in the central foyer stairway modelled in revolutionary Constructivist style

# NATIONAL MUSEUM, TIANANMEN SQUARE, BEIJING

In planning

Of the over one hundred projects gmp have designed for China this must be the most politically sensitive. The National Museum site on Tiananmen Square is the most prominent in the nation and considering its cultural importance it is surprising that a foreign architect has been chosen. However, this decision is in line with China's policy of collecting international stars to add lustre to their new found economic power and gmp architects have proved their tenacity and reliability in China since the late nineties.

The existing fifties, Soviet-style structure, combining both the Chinese History Museum and Museum of the Revolution, acts as a counterweight on the east side of the square to the Great Hall of the People, the Chinese government building, on the west of the square. This museum rehabilitation project will unify the two theme museums and the former common grand entrance will make way for a more transparent and inviting 'Grand Forum' which should be able to accommodate at least 5,000 people at any one time, underlining the open and public nature of this depository of Chinese history. More than 15,000 visitors are expected daily. Beyond the requirements of the original brief the architects see the 'Grand Forum' as a venue for ceremonies and official occasions, additional to its function as leisure space with catering, museum shop and information centre. Grandiose symmetrical order is the planning concept using ceremonial stairways, ramps, and podiums, and a new light well rising as a monumental red core to a cantilevered roof over the whole museum.

From the existing western courtyard of the old building the broad stairway will be match by stepped water basins to ameliorate the hot summer temperatures but most visitors will enter the Forum through the new north portico and benches included in the stair design will provide seating for group tours and their guides. Openings carved out of the Forum floor will give views down into the 14,400 square metres of the Special Display area. In keeping with these exhibits as archaeological finds the perforated floor represents excavation digs. The basement positioning of the Special Display and museum storage in a second basement offers the best security for these priceless items. The Forum itself will be the stage for plays of light with a reflective ceiling mirroring activities in the light well during the day and at night, when the exhibition halls are closed, video beamers set into the floor will project text, films and light effects, in a multimedia composition.

The two existing museum wings will be improved with multiple access points and connection to the Forum and a new

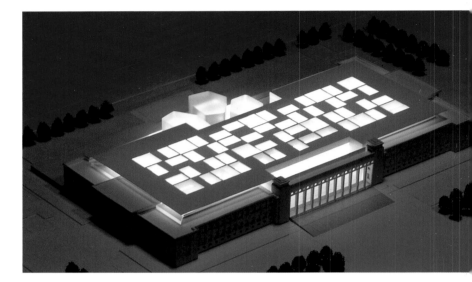

The museum modernization and remodelling bows to Tiananmen Square's prevailing state architecture

Museum Garden on the East side. Three amorphic structures containing an Academic Reporting Hall, Ceremonial Hall and Digital Cinema, breaking out of the formal museum block into a small lake, will be an added attraction. Work stations in a separate wing for administrators, visiting scholars and researchers, will overlook two green landscaped courtyards.

Sensational architectural gestures are inappropriate here where the Museum remodelling subsumes itself to the overall greater whole of its location. The eaves level of the new roof will be 34.50 metres to match the Great Hall of the People and improve the spatial and volumetric relationship between these two important structures on opposite sides of Tiananmen Square. Bronze cladding of the new roof terrace has been chosen to match the many historical exhibits within the building and when

glimpsed from the square it will have a matt golden appearance but, in order not to compete with the roofs of the Imperial Palace, the external cladding will weather to a darker shade. The General Display on view at roof level is conceived as a more entertaining presentation of exhibits and combines with the 'live' historical buildings in the panoramic view of the Square. Tiananmen Square's night time illuminations are already impressive in their power symbolism but the flood-lighting of the newly refurbished Museum promises to even further impress upon the public the weight of such a long and turbulent national history.

Unsurprisingly, in a land of ever inflating statistics the increased 170,000 square metres gross floor area will make China's National Museum the largest in the world.

gmp von Gerkan, Marg und Partner

# MUSEUM ARCHIVES AND EXHIBITION HALL FOR URBAN DEVELOPMENT, PUDONG, SHANGHAI

Completion 2005

The Chinese, justifiably proud of their building, architectural and planning achievements within a very short time frame, are documenting and collecting material to fill several museums. The Urban Development Exhibition Centre in Shanghai's Renmin Park already attracts thousands of foreign tourists, the Chinese public and professionals. The competition for an Archives Museum in the new Pudong business district across the Huangpu River, was won by gmp in 2002 and will be an even grander temple-like construction.

Occupying a complete city block the gross floor area of 41,000 square metres will be contained in a floating cube and marginal side block raised above street level on a stepped podium of gigantic proportions. Archives will be stored within the four-metre-high podium structure while administration offices will be housed in the parallel wing on the east side of the site, leaving the square cube for public presentations, exhibitions on ongoing developments and Shanghai's historical developments.

The base level of the cube is a transparent space, clad in full height glass and functioning as introductory foyer with vertical access to the exhibitions in the 'floating' volume. This upper section is more solid in appearance with an outer sheath of glass and an inner skin of movable panelled walls which can be either fully closed to the elevation or opened up for views into and out of the exhibitions. For the passing public the façade is intended to function as an information wall with micro and macro graphics and images, films or text, projected from beamers mounted within the wall construction.

When completed the Museum of Archives promises to be on a comparable scale to the over dimensioned developments it wants to promote, nationally and internationally.

**Like a Greco-Roman classical temple, the archives are elevated on a stepped podium, symbolising their importance as national treasures**

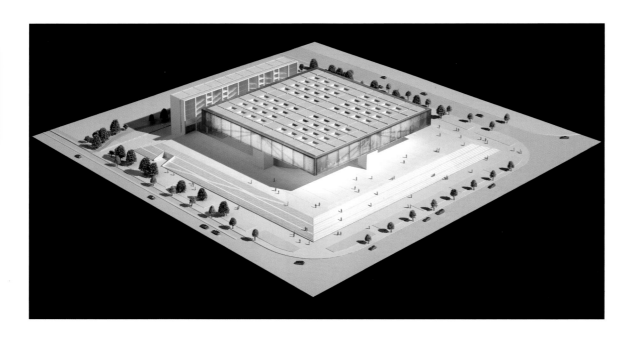

# MUSEUM AND ART GALLERY, TSINGHUA UNIVERSITY, BEIJING

In planning

Tsinghua University, in the north-west of Beijing, was founded in 1911 on the grounds of a former Qing Dynasty royal garden. Financed by the Boxer Indemnity money it started as a school for students who would later be sent by the government for further studies in the US. By 1925 it had a university level and in 1952, under the newly established People's Republic, it became a polytechnic university with emphasis on engineering. Since 1978 it has been adding other faculties and in 1999 the School of Arts and Design merged with the Central Academy of Arts and Design. New development targets, planned for the next fifteen years, are in line with a national policy of Education Reform.

As part of the university's aim to strengthen the arts and humanities the new Museum and Art Gallery is planned for a site on the eastern boundary of the campus, opposite the school of Art and Design. A new east-west thoroughfare, as defined in the city urban plan, will divide the future campus of the academy of arts and design into two parts.

Like the architect's previous work the design is both dramatic and solid and in this case a red natural stone is planned for the façade cladding, alternating with setback glazed areas to provide shadow for the windows. The structure of the upper floor gallery will cantilever over the museum at ground level like a huge protecting porch. At the front of the museum an expansive public area is to be landscaped with soft and hard features, plants, trees and stone finishes.

On the approach to the entrance, and protected by the overhanging porch, there will be an area available for open air exhibitions and, through the entrance lobby, direct access to an internal unroofed courtyard for sculpture. In the gallery above, for both permanent and temporary exhibitions, the ceiling will be eight metres high and the floor area planned on an 8.1 metre modular grid. The roof is to act as a large filter for a zenith natural light with planting on the eaves perimeter to ameliorate the microclimate. Gallery and museum lighting for the exhibits will come from mixed, natural and artificial, sources.

On two intermediate levels lounges and a multimedia gallery will have a panoramic view over the campus. All services and support functions are to be grouped in a five storey block at the rear of the building with staff rooms, loading dock facilities, security control, storage, workshops, and curators offices connecting back into the public areas.

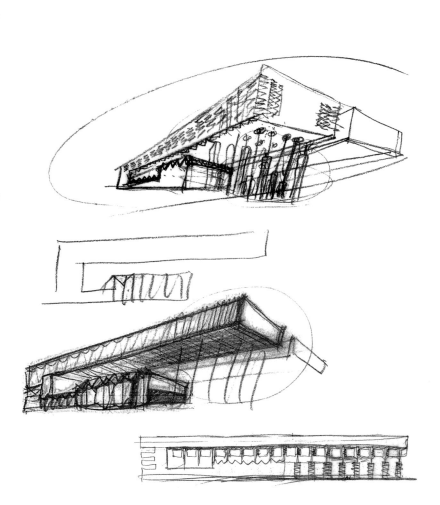

In a geometrical play of proportions, voids and solids, the gallery is a
piece of modernist sculpture in its own right

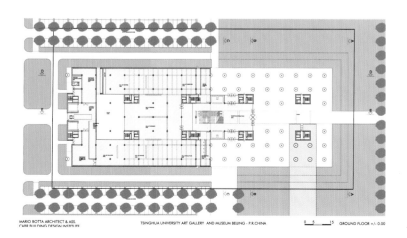

MARIO BOTTA ARCHITECT & ASS.
CABB BUILDING DESIGN INSTITUTE
TSINGHUA UNIVERSITY ART GALLERY AND MUSEUM BEIJING - P.R.CHINA
0  5    15    GROUND FLOOR +/- 0.00

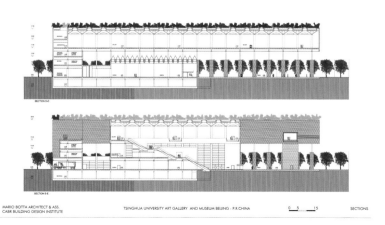

MARIO BOTTA ARCHITECT & ASS.
CABB BUILDING DESIGN INSTITUTE
TSINGHUA UNIVERSITY ART GALLERY AND MUSEUM BEIJING - P.R.CHINA
0  5    15    SECTIONS

# CULTURE COMPLEX, SHUNDE NEW CITY

In planning

Shunde City is an ancient foundation located near the mouth of the Pearl river where it flows into the Pacific. It has a harbour and faces Shenzhen, the South Chinese economic hot spot, across the estuary. Shunde has good highway links to both the Guangdong provincial capital, Guangzhou, to the North, and to Macau, the former Portuguese colony, on the southern seaboard.

This cultural complex, on a 120,000-square-metre site in the centre of Shunde's New City, has the difficult task of creating an immediate sense of location and belonging where none existed before. Remo Riva, P&T director and architect of the scheme, described it as 'new buildings in paddy fields'. This is not a unique problem in contemporary China where instant cities are springing up like weeds around the kernels of ancient and traditional settlements, or being built on green field sites where only the trading conditions of a Special Economic Zone reign.

What are termed 'signature' buildings will form the core of this urban group; museum, library, opera house and science museum. Using water, patches of land and human scale, the architect has woven an artificial landscape around the structures. In comparison to attempts in many other cities this new urban heart has been designed as a poetic *gesamtwerk*, rising out of a shallow lake, with islands like water lily leaves. A formal frame of trees will replace the traditional enclave perimeter wall. Eastern influences can be traced in the garden layout, gateway towers, and 'big poster' window frames and graphics, matched with slick post modern buildings displaying plenty of what the Americans might call 'attitude'.

At the end of 2004 there were plans to start building the first phase including conference hall, library and opera house.

**Post-modernism was embraced by Chinese architects as a way to integrate traditional Chinese and western modern forms. Where architecture must conjure up its own context it is still seen as a useful design vehicle.**

# INTERCONFESSIONAL PRAYER HALL, ZHANG JIANG HI-TECH PARK, PUDONG, SHANGHAI

In planning

The strategy of founding hi-tech parks, as seedbeds for new initiatives, has produced a rash of satellite centres across China run by new town corporations. Placed close to the most important metropoles to benefit from any synergetic effects and provided with new buildings, facilities and highly-qualified staff, these hot-beds of pioneering activity in the applied sciences have the task of catching up with and overtaking all previous achievements in the older industrialized world. Zhang Jiang is one of the most important because of its proximity to China's most developed westernised mega-city, Shanghai. Expectations are enormous but perhaps not unrealistic. Inhabitants and workers will mainly be of Chinese origin, many of whom have been educated abroad, and former emigrants who have returned, attracted by the new working opportunities, in cooperation with foreign multinational firms, research and academic institutions. The atmosphere will be, by definition, international.

New arrivals will expect modern, synonymous with 'western', standards in housing, shopping and recreational choices. These multinational serviced towns with their global outlook could not be more distant from the agriculture based villages, in which most of China's population still live, if they were on the moon. In these elitist and protected nodes, the official openness and tolerance of new ideas in the pursuit of prosperity does not stop at science. A broad band of spiritual needs are also to be satisfied.

The design of Zhang Jiang's Hi-Tech Park Prayer Hall won first prize in the competition for a congregational building for 1,200–1,500 worshippers on a site near the river. Neutrality was required to embrace all faiths and the elliptical, egg-like, plan does not have a strong directional focus based on any one religion. Rows of seats are accommodated in the body of the hall and there is a mezzanine and balcony level. Like an onion the structure has an outer roofed loggia which encircles the building, an encircling internal corridor sandwiched between the outer translucent wall of glass and an opaque and solid internal wall which acoustically and visually protects the core area for meditation and prayer.

The full height, glazed curtain wall of the enclosure hangs from the structural frame of the roof, a gridiron system of fish-bellied beams, stiffened by truss rods in two directions and clad in tinted glass. The external, thin, concrete-slab canopy to the loggia is supported on slender columns. The composition of weightlessness and soaring height should evoke the idea of a sparkling jewel with the help of reflected light from the sky and nearby water.

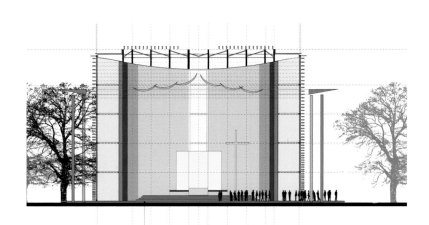

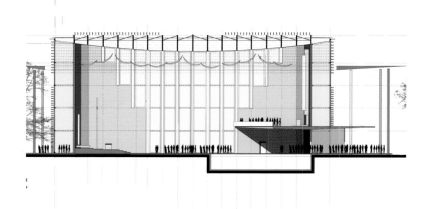

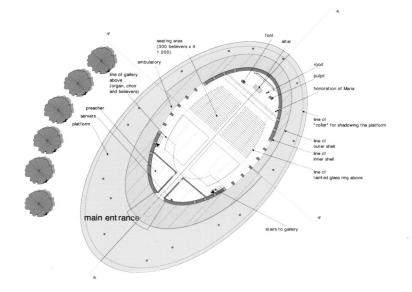

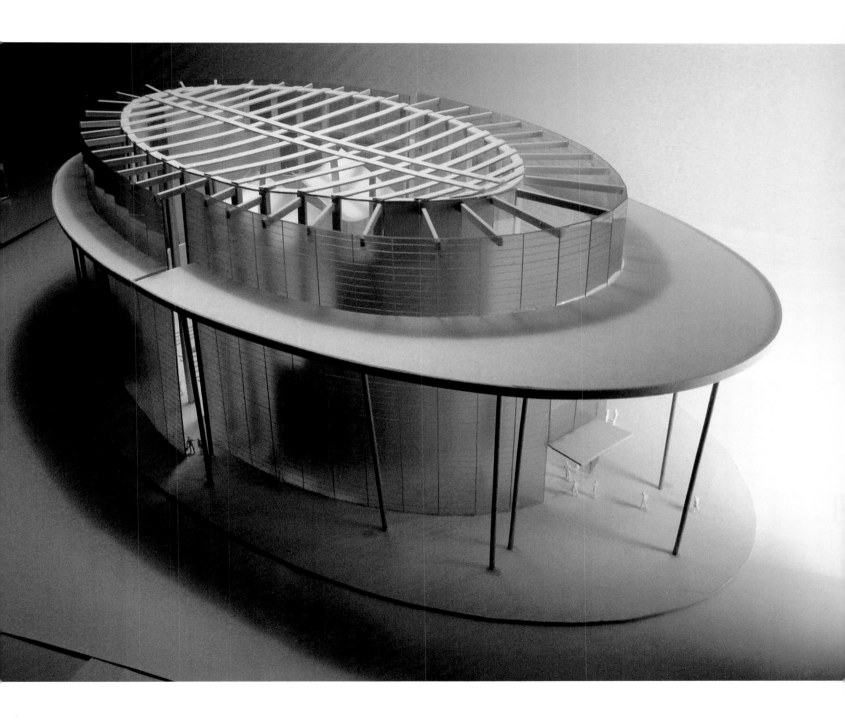

△ A modest piece of architecture which manages to avoid stepping on any sensitivities and can be used as a temple, chapel, mosque or free-thinkers meeting house. The universality of mankind does not need a pompous pulpit.

Paul Andreu

# GUANGZHOU GYMNASIUM, GUANGZHOU

Completion 2001

This 100,000-square-metre sports centre, on an eight-hectare site which is in turn integrated into an eighteen-hectare park with other sports grounds, was one of the main venues for China's ninth National Games in 2001. It could be said to have been a practice run, in construction and organization, for the much bigger Olympic events in 2008.

Located to the north-east of the former international airport it forms a transition between the city and surrounding nature reserves of the Baiyun Hills. The three, white, undulating roofed shells mirror their hilly surroundings and are partially embedded in the site. Their playing arenas are set below external ground levels so that spectators entering the buildings walk down to the bleachers. Athletes have separate entrances, linked to their sports village and training centre

Each shell has a different function. The main stadium is flexible enough to host athletic events with 6,500 seated spectators, or smaller staged events like gymnastics, team sports, tennis and table-tennis with up to 10,000 spectators. This hall can also hold big show entertainments. The second shell is for training with an Olympic sized pool and designated rooms for other disciplines. The third shell is an open public sports centre. Around this triathlon configuration there are the usual, unavoidable, hectares of car parking, administration offices, and the athlete's village with a restaurant designed by other architects. Roof cladding is semi-transparent pearly white, supported on a lightweight steel frame designed to withstand seismic movement in an earthquake area. Internally the architect succeeded in producing a warm white natural light which does not dazzle. He places great emphasis on the fact that this milky soft light quality does not over dramatize sport, or contribute to creating a violent, tension ridden, atmosphere. The result is a quality of light which is also conducive to television filming.

When completed in 2001 the Gymnasium was the first project of architectural quality in Guangzhou, the capital city of a province which was just beginning to gather economic momentum. Four years later the city has commissioned a new river side cultural centre with opera house and museum, designed respectively by Zaha Hadid and Rocco Yim, to crown their commercial success.

**A multi-purpose main stadium for 6,500 or 10,000 seated spectators**

Three shell-like stadium roofs nestle into the rolling landscape of the Baiyun Hills

1 Main Hall
2 Training Hall
3 Maa Sport Center
4 Athletes Village
5 Administration Building
6 Parking
7 Restaurant
8 Garden

Sasaki Associates Inc.

# OLYMPIC GREEN, BEIJING

Individual projects to be completed 2008

Olympic Green is the landscaped setting for the principal events during the 2008 Beijing Olympics. In July 2002 Sasaki Associates convinced the international competition jury with their master plan and later won 20,000 public votes during an exhibition of finalist's designs. As with any large master plan there were dissenting opinions on the practicality of the scheme. The *China Daily* of 27 July 2002 reported that Lan Tianzhu, the director of the cultural, health and sports subcommittee, doubted as to whether water resources would be adequate when he saw the proposed water system covering more than 100 hectares. "It will possibly become a stinking open basin if there is insufficient water or if it becomes stagnant after the Olympics," he warned. Shanjixiang, the director of the Planning Committee, who rejected this criticism, said the amount of water used by industry and agriculture in Beijing had decreased, while the volume assigned for environmental use was expected to rise in 2002 to 400 million cubic metres. Moreover, the Beijing water situation would benefit from the trans-regional south to north water-transfer project being completed for the 2008 Olympics and only recycled water was to be used for planting and irrigation.

At the North end of the Olympic Green, the 700-hectare, 'natural' ecological Forest Park will be home to multiple biotopes, three types of wetlands, meadows and upland forests, and help increase bio-diversity in the urban centre. Progressing south the Cultural Axis, which highlights the achievements of China's great historical dynasties over 5,000 years, flows into the Olympic Axis, which is flanked by the new sports venues. These include the existing Asian Games stadium, the new National Stadium, designed by Herzog & de Meuron, and the National Swimming Centre designed by PTW Architects with CSCEC and Arup Group. The complete Central Axis, linking all these sections, runs from Tiananmen Square and the Forbidden City in the south to Forest Park in the north. The framework for the layout of this entire central zone is the existing city grid which covers the four-kilometre-long tract. The scale is monumental and the Central Axis itself overpowering in its dynamic cut through the landscape.

From the south a pedestrian approach starts at the Olympic Gate and runs in a straight processional line northwards beside the Olympic Way with its flags of competing nations. The Olympic entry section continues this northern route with a commemorative site leading into the cluster of major stadiums. The southern tail end of Forest Lake embraces the National Stadium and

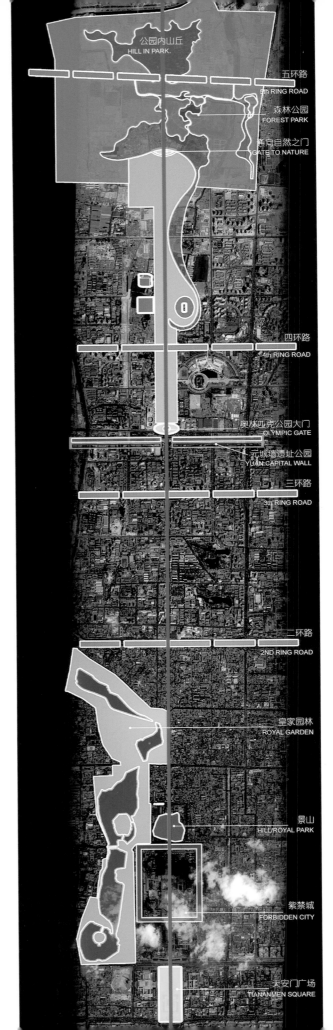

then snakes northward to enclose several decorative rock islands providing habitats for wild fauna and flora. Along the axis there are squares, a fountain and possible open air Olympic Gallery. A transport node and more cultural sites are planned along the northern stretch of the axis which terminates at Forest Park Square. Here an elliptical amphitheatre can stage major civic gatherings and performing arts.

Incorporating the three Olympic ideals, sports, culture and environment, this planning concept aims to achieve urban balance and integration, between east and west, technology and nature, historical and modern times. Conceived as a poetic narrative Forest Park symbolizes the cradle of Chinese civilization with water flowing from its artificial lake southward into a canal which runs alongside the green borders of the central axis. The ecological aspects of the plan are considered pivotal in the later development of a sustainable urban environment, with green lungs and public sports facilities. A further educational aim is to reintroduce indigenous wild life into the city and give ordinary citizens a chance to experience 'nature'.

For the Olympic National Stadium at the heart of the Olympic Green, designs by Herzog & de Meuron, working with the China Architecture Design Institute, the Beijing Architecture Design Institute, and AXS of Japan with Tsinghua University Architecture Design Institute, were picked from a total of forty-four entries by the international competition jury. An exhibition at the Beijing International Convention Center in March 2003

◁　**The north-south orientated Olympic Green site plan**

▽　**Aerial view with the distinctive Herzog & de Meuron National Stadium**

attracted 6,000 visitors, of whom 3,506 voted for the Herzog & de Meuron and China Architecture Design Institute's design.

The competition entry had a series of raked 1.5 metre-deep, steel box girders sixty-seven metres high which criss-crossed, giving the impression of woven twigs. Early in the process Herzog & de Meuron consulted with Beijing artist Ai Weiwei, known for his Dadaist attitudes and, for Chinese sensibilities, provocative ideas on value and authenticity in Chinese culture. Ai Weiwei encouraged the architects to develop the crazy, chaotic structure of the stadium and first sketched a tree and a bird's nest, both classical Chinese poetic images, to illustrate his concept.

The façade and structure were originally designed to be identical. An invisible membrane of inflated cushions, as the stadium's weatherproof skin, was to fill the openings between girders. Inside the bowl stadium there should be no visible structure to hinder the 100,000 spectators sightlines. Visitors would enter through a covered foyer with restaurants and shops from which a spacious concourse would then open out with stands in three, unbroken, continuous tiers, reinforcing the impression of a simple bowl. According to the architects: "The crowd is the architecture." In bad weather a translucent membrane roof with a grid structure was intended to slide across the sky. Placed on a gentle rise in the Olympic Green landscape the stadium was conceived as a 'collective bowl', an image which sits well in the land of rice bowls with a recent ideology of communal sharing.

This is just one of the many architectural projects which have been affected by the criticism of the Chinese government over inappropriate spending on over-dimensioned national gestures. In August 2004 work was stopped for a financial audit of the design. The original budget was reported in the Peoples Daily 23/8/04 to have been reduced by deleting the retractable roof, enlarging the size of the roof top opening and so reducing the amount of latticework steel construction. To what extent the structure's original visual impact has been diluted remains to be seen.

Burckhardt + Partner

# 2008 OLYMPICS WUKESONG CULTURAL AND SPORTS CENTER, BEIJING

Completion 2007

This is not just one stadium but a complex in which 30% of the area will be maintained as parkland and market gardens. Three basic concepts have been united; that of Green spaces including orchards and vegetable gardens, the hi-tech Olympics with giant façade screens as multimedia attractions, and the idea of the People's Olympics in which the actual layout of the grounds invite the public to assemble, wander around and take part. There is a strong pedagogical message here linking physical activities with healthy eating for a healthy life.

In July 2002 Sasaki Associates and Burckhardt + Partner tied for second prize. A first prize was not awarded. However, during the following fourteen-day exhibition attended by 50,000 members of the public, contrary to the experts choice, most votes went to the Canadian entry by ABCP working with the Beijing Urban Architecture Design Institute, which Chen Jianjun of the Beijing Municipal City Planning Committee had said 'lacked feasibility'. In true Chinese style a compromise was reached. "We will adopt the advantages of this design as much as possible as an act of respecting audiences opinions," commented Chen Jianjun (30/7/02 China Daily). Winners were eventually Burckhardt + Partner.

The layout is based on a grid of crater-like indentations in the landscape. Different activities, such as the basketball hall, temporary baseball and softball fields, or future facilities such as the indoor swimming complex, or botanical gardens with labelled indigenous and foreign imported plants can be allotted to each crater. The elevated grid of avenues and paths dividing the craters allows a panoramic view over the site for pedestrians who can move freely through the centre, while concentric rings are dedicated to vehicular traffic. Private cars are to be prohibited within

the innermost ring. Changes of use within the crater-plots can take place without overturning the upper level network of circulation systems and superficial appearance of an agrarian landscape.

The Wukesong Multipurpose Sports Hall is one of the structures integrated into the crater grid. During the Olympics gigantic outdoor screens, accessible to all, will show live events. There will be an outdoor summer cinema, space to lounge and relax, bleacher benches for open-air concerts and spaces for spontaneous entertainment. Internally the hall has an upper level for business and entertainment, information desk, hotel, fitness studios, sports clubs, commerce and catering, and a lower level for the multipurpose stadium. A wide range of sports can be accommodated from the Olympic basketball games to handball, hockey, soccer, roller skating, volleyball, table tennis and non-sports such as conferences, receptions and concerts.

The hall's dramatic roof structure is a series of twelve, suspended, hyperbolic paraboloids hanging from the main ring of steel girders which in turn support all the functions at the upper level. It is intended that the geometry and orientation of the building will help save on energy for heating and air-conditioning. The hyperbolic paraboloids should act as chimneys drawing external air from the lower levels and expelling used air through the roof.

Passive, energy-saving market gardening and the teaching element in the botanical garden is very much in line with latest policy statements from the government on a more ecological and people orientated development. It will be interesting to observe whether these concepts, conceived in Europe, will work in a Beijing winter when the infamous, dust laden, winds blow across the capital.

▽ **Section through the hyperbolic paraboloids**

▷ **Elevations as big poster art**

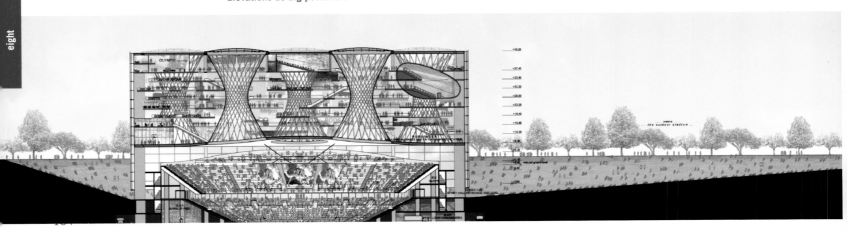

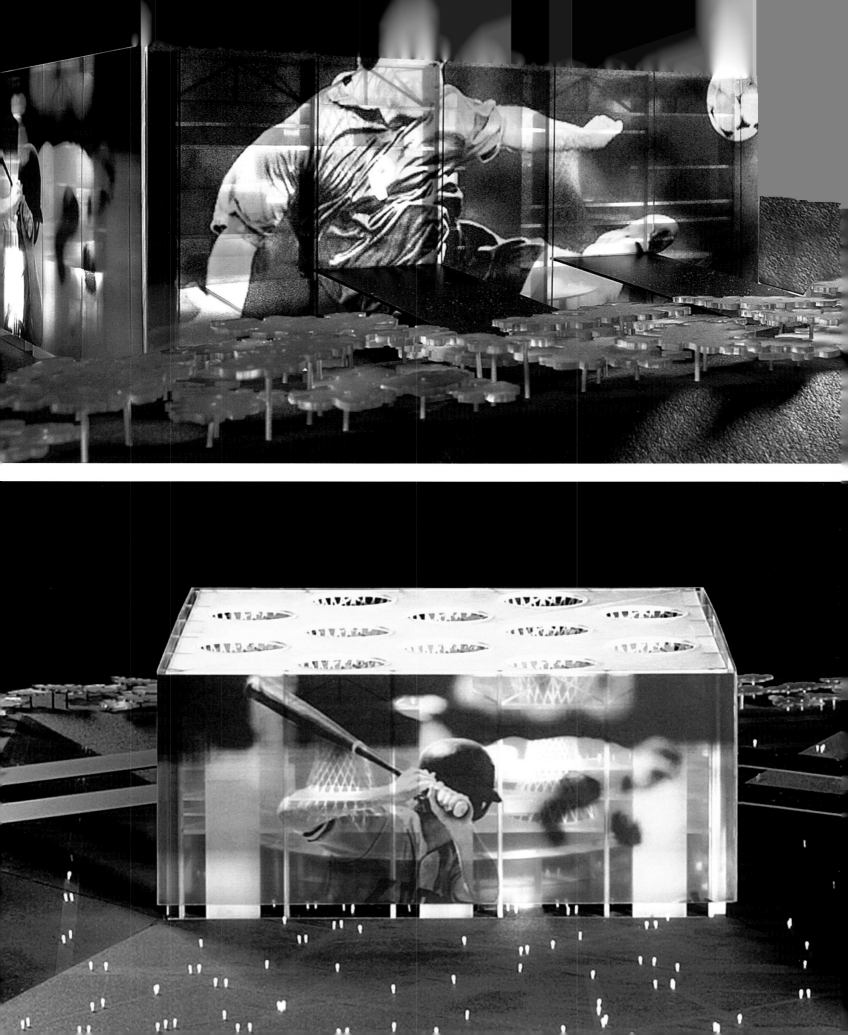

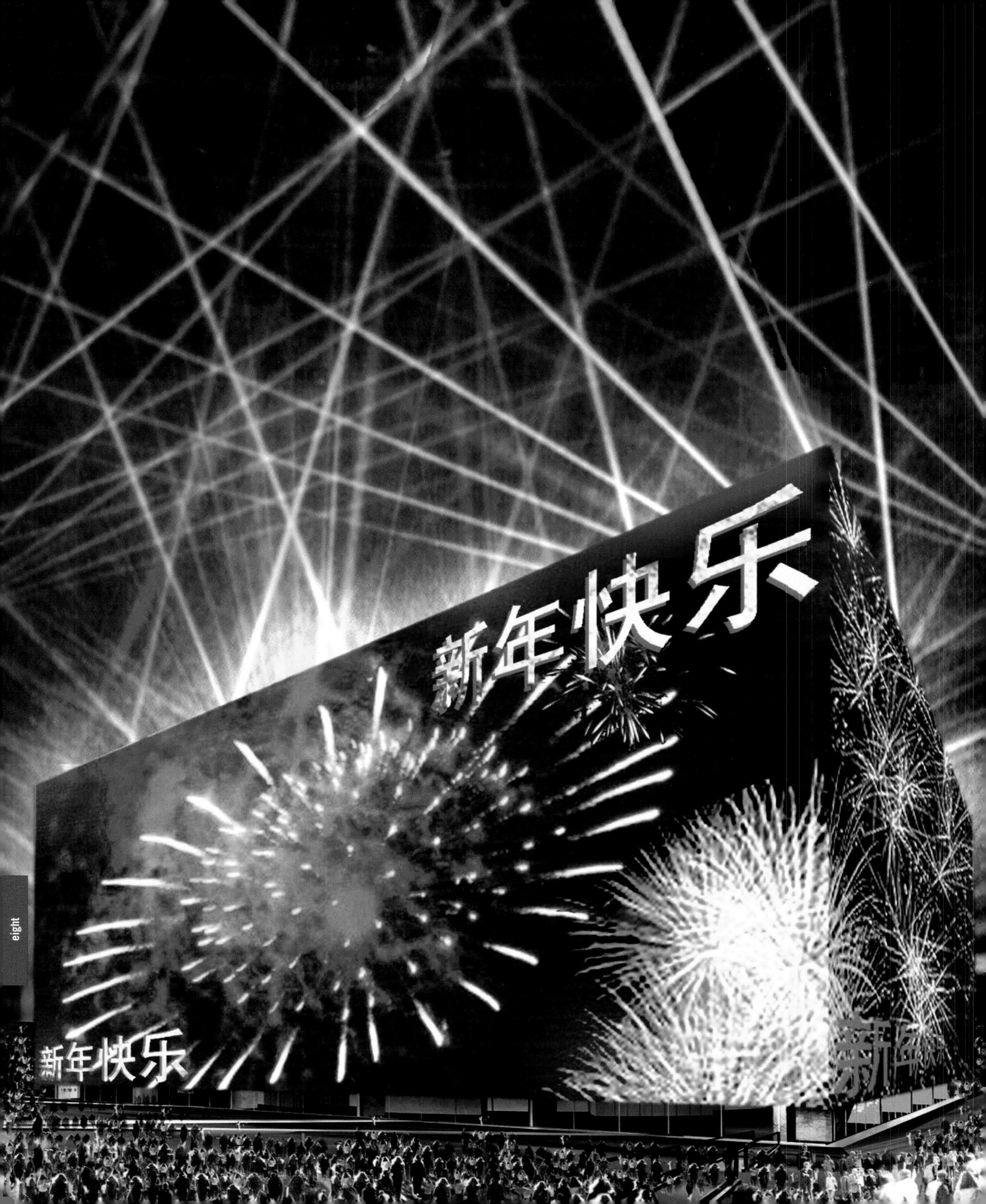
新年快乐
新年快乐

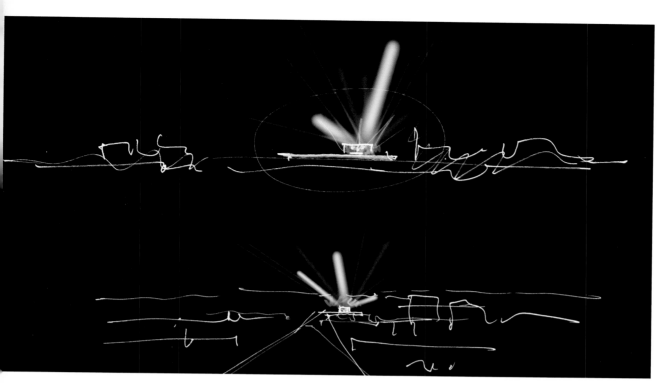

Sport venues as spectacles and entertainment in themselves, without sport

AS&P Albert Speer & Partner

# ANTING INTERNATIONAL AUTOMOBILE CITY AND NEW TOWN, ANTING, SHANGHAI

In planning and construction since 2000

In the 1980s Volkswagen built their first Chinese assembly plant in Anting, twenty-five kilometres north-west of the centre of Shanghai. Building on this foundation China decided to develop an International Automobile City, connected to an expanded Anting new town, as the centre of the nation's future automobile industry. Ten square kilometres will be dedicated to the automobile city alone, with manufacturing, exhibition, trade, research and development, management and training buildings and services. Spin-off requirements, for offices, hotels, restaurants, shops, entertainment and a leisure park, are also part of the master plan along with a city for 30,000 inhabitants, most of whom will find employment in the automobile related activities.

This is urban planning on a grand scale with many planning blocks fitting into a web of interactive needs. After winning the design competition for the whole region AS&P were asked to complete a master plan for Anting and an urban development plan for the automobile city. In a second stage the core of the trade and exhibition zone was developed with the grouping of high-rise towers, to define the city skyline, and lower level buildings melting into the natural landscape.

Anting New Town is to have all the characteristics and standards of an ideal German city, it's layout based on a medieval walled market town but filled in with contemporary building forms and detailing. When it comes to a leading edge auto-mobile industry there is to be no pretence of a Chinese style modernism. Located between the Wusong River and the Shanghai Nanjing highway it is an autark island, like a fortress city surrounded by a moat. At the centre there is to be a town square, with smaller squares and parks spilling out into the neigh-bourhoods. The Central Plaza Hotel of 30,000 square metres at the west side of this central square will have all the expected services of a representational international hotel, with 240 guest rooms and thirty-five suites, all contained in a modern building of classical proportions with a roof extending over the pedestrian way forming a covered arcade along one side of the plaza. A fifty-nine-metre-high hotel campanile tower, with public access to an observation platform overlooking the city, is to mark the town centre. In the absence of a real church as the focal point of an historical European city commerce takes over this identification function. Radiating from the central square, high streets are to be flanked by five-storey blocks, gradually stepping down to four and three storeys further from the centre. A ribbon of water of changing width runs through the centre of the town from one side of the surrounding moat to the other.

The idea of recreating a German town in China, a 72,000-square-metre patch of Europe in Asia, is itself a copy of the first German colonialists buildings in places like Tsingtao, now spelt Qingdao, where Germans founded the Tsingtao brewery. If modernization is considered identical with westernisation then the one to one relationship is taken to an even higher level. In the absence of an indigenous modern vocabulary China reaches back into its history with the 'foreign barbarians' and remembers the German colonial efficiency, order and reliability. To be copied is a form of flattery but while the use of trusted forms may short cut development it does nothing for an analysis of a unique locality. What about microclimate, topography and culture? But, if form follows function and the functions of manufacturing and twenty-first century urban life are universally identical why should a town in China look any different from one in Germany? Chinese, one-child families and affluent singles are well on the way to having western-cloned lifestyles.

▽  **Anting New Town as an ideal German city**

▷  **A medieval walled market city layout, but filled with contemporary architecture**

21号塔式住宅二层平面
21 - first floor

21号塔式住宅三层平面
21 - second floor

21号塔式住宅四层平面
21 - third floor

21号塔式住宅五层平面
21 - fourth floor

21号塔式住宅六层平面
21 - fifth floor

21号塔式住宅七层平面
21 - sixth floor

21号塔式住宅屋顶平面
21 - roofgarden

21号塔楼各层平面
Tower Building 21
Floor plans

nine

Behnisch, Behnisch & Partner

# ANTING NEW TOWN NEIGHBOURHOOD, ANTING, SHANGHAI

In planning

▽ **Apartment blocks in a global green suburbia**

Proposals for various Anting New Town neighbourhoods were commissioned from several German architects. This one is to include both medium rise apartment towers, kindergarten and sports complex. The client's request for 'individuality' suggests a marketing ploy. Functionality is taken for granted. What the prospective new middle-class families and singles want are life styles, new self images in modern outfits, which fit with their new economic base and future aspirations. There is no street life, in the traditional sense of public life, and no hierarchy of external private space, yards or gardens, giving way to public pavement and thoroughfare. Family or personal lives take place behind closed doors and the boundary between personal and public is abrupt, completely at variance with Chinese living conditions only twenty-five years ago. The model is privatised, Western European modernism developed out of American suburbia.

All apartment plans are based on the same system, a vertical service shaft and similar basic modules. External visual interest is created by turning each apartment layout through several degrees so that the towers do not appear to be stacks of identical units.

The sports complex consists of three major buildings grouped to form a single identity. An extensively contoured and sculptured park landscape sets the sports activities apart from the residential neighbourhood. Landscaped 'natural' features should dominate the overall impression so that the sloped metal roofs of buildings look as though they are continuations of grassed slopes. Entry to the sports hall is raised 4.5 metres above the surrounding playing fields and swimming pools for a panoramic overview. An awkward division of the site by a main road is overcome with a low flying footbridge treated as an integral continuation of the landscape on both sides.

Suburban neighbourhood sports facilities
grassed over as natural landscape features

立面
功能馆
est Elevation
orts Complex

orth 北

泳池馆/ Natatorium/ Swimming Pool

体育馆 Sports Hall

多功能馆 Multi Hall

南 South

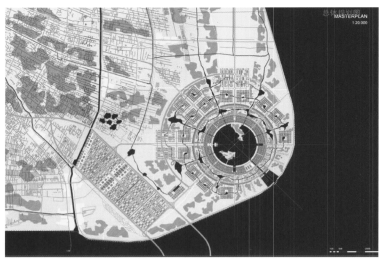

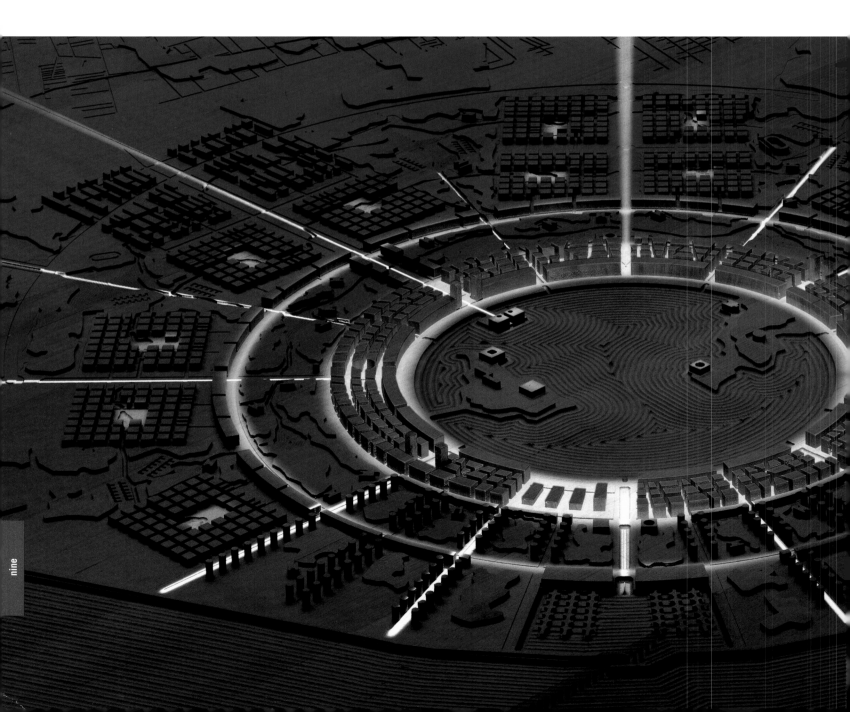

gmp von Gerkan, Marg und Partner

# LUCHAO HARBOUR CITY, SHANGHAI

In planning

**Luchao's Harbour City's lake, with a diameter of twenty-five kilometres, will be a prominent feature on the coastal headland**

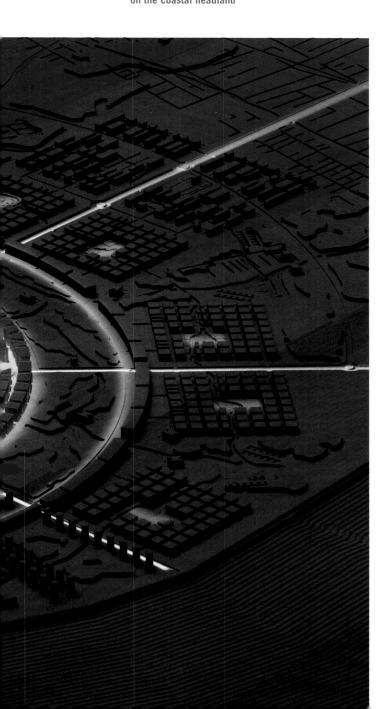

Subtitled a 'Metropolis in the East China Sea' the new, sixty-five-square-kilometre, Shanghai satellite town of Luchao includes the international, deep-sea container harbour Yangshan. Shanghai is now the largest container terminal in the world and Luchao Harbour City will house 300,000 of the projected sixteen million Shanghai Metropolitan inhabitants by the year 2020. To give some idea of the scale of this development Luchao claims to be in the same league as Chandigarh, Brasilia and Canberra, similar mammoth urban settlements built in the last hundred years.

Like Hamburg, where the architects have their head-quarters, the central feature of Luchao is to be a man made lake. Slightly larger than Hamburg's Alster lake the Chinese version will have a 2.5 kilometre diameter and eight kilometres of waterside promenade with 'la Copa Cabana' bathing beach and boat transport to various islands dedicated to culture and leisure activities. Client representatives were apparently very impressed by their Hamburg visit and decided to take home a bigger and better version of Hanseatic lifestyle, with the advantages of a subtropical climate, as souvenir.

Although modelled on the ideals of the traditional European city, meaning presumably the importance of democratic govern-ment, art and music institutions, education and citizens housing, the Chinese version also differs in being symmetrically ordered. Concentric circles of zoned uses spread out from the lake, like ripples from an epicentre, meeting both the Chinese fondness for marshalled neatness and allegory. A 500-metre-wide ring of city park will be the setting for individually placed public buildings and enclose inner rings of shopping pedestrian areas and densely packed business and commercial developments. Within the third ring fourteen housing segments will be self-sufficient communities with shops, social services, clinics and schools for all age groups. A radial pattern of roads, for private vehicles and a light railway system, and canals, for water supply and recreation, superimposed on the circular plan will create a hierarchy of graduated wedges, allow variations in character, but also make clear the unity of the overall plan. A micro scale of public squares, pockets of landscaping, small lakes, and intruding wedges of outlying countryside, are to be included to help individualization and identification of neighbourhoods.

Human life is not conducive to mathematical regulation, as a visit to Chandigarh six decades after Le Corbusier's master-planning shows, but the ring and radial concept does allow for growth in line with the original concept.

Luchao will be on a scale comparable to India's Chandigarh,
Brazil's Brasilia and Australia's Canberra

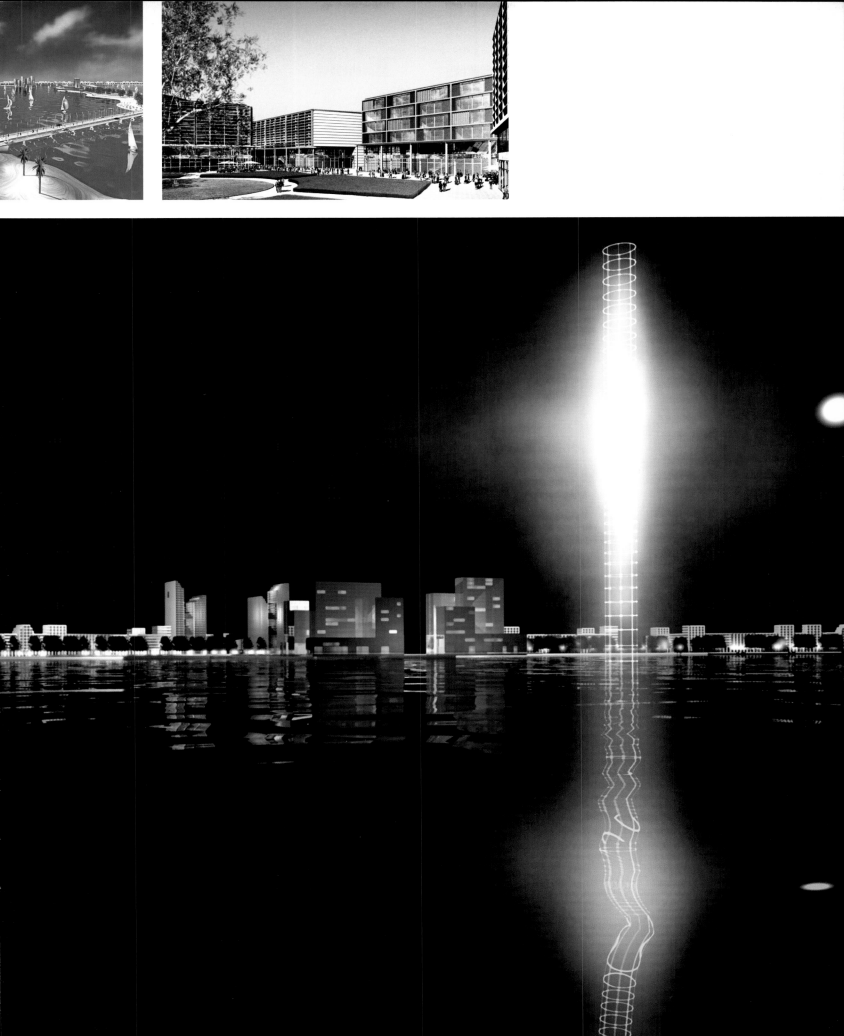

# BOAO CANAL VILLAGE, HAINAN ISLAND
Completed 2002

Boao village, on the island of Hainan at the most southern point of China, takes it's design inspiration from historic river settlements, such as Wuzhen or Zhouzhuang, clustered alongside rivers and canals. In Tang poetry they were described as "human dwellings entwined by green water."

But this is a contemporary residential development of 400 houses, from 200 to 400 square metres in area, for families living in the twenty-first century. The architects have avoided the use of second-hand, traditional details, moon gates or arched stone bridges, while managing to re-create the same traditional ambience of tranquillity and frugality. The shallow river is the focus of views from the terraces of water front houses and the place for community and family sport, transport, or peaceful solitude.

There are white-washed walls and stone-paved courtyards but the architecture is modern with passive energy-saving and ecologically-friendly systems employed to blend in with the natural environment. Care has been taken to conserve the level, quality and flow of water, existing biotopes, vegetation, landforms and wildlife habitats. Orientation of the housing units takes advantage of cooling breezes in summer and protects against typhoon winds. Cross ventilation by induction reduces the need for air-conditioning. Solar panels generate power and heat water to make the settlement semi-independent of external power stations. Newly-constructed canals have been linked to the river system to make boats a preferable option to cars, which means less noise and air pollution.

Rocco Yim, the Hong Kong architect, becomes quite lyrical when he compares Boao Canal Village to the Land of Peach Blossoms, a Chinese folklore utopia where the inhabitants were oblivious of distant dynasties and changes in government.

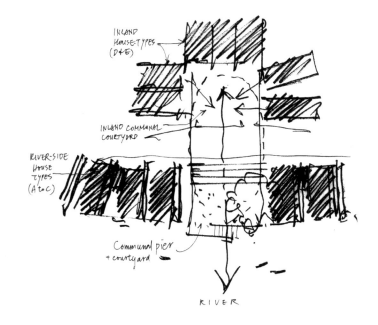

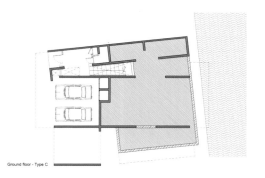

Ground floor - Type C

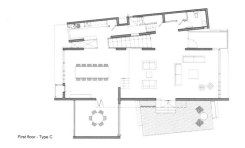

First floor - Type C

Second floor - Type C

Boao Canal Village houses, main living room windows and private gardens relate to the water with a small public terraced square also leading down to the water

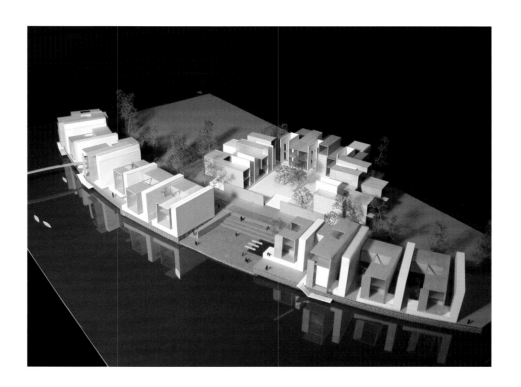

3rd floor - Type C

White washed villas and discreet private spaces, under a sub-tropical sun, are comparable with Mediteranean coastal settlements.

# PHOENIX CITY, SUZHOU
Competition Entry 2004

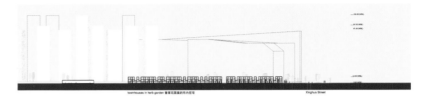

site section west - east to the north of Gangtian Road
俯-路东西向到北向的基地剖面 1:1000

The layout of this new town for 300,000 residents, looking like a game of snakes and blobs, is situated beside the Xietang River and to the east of Lake Jinji. Suzhou, the ancient city renowned for its classical gardens, lies to the West and the modern Suzhou Industrial Park to the east. Easily accessible from Shanghai by train this region is agriculturally and culturally fertile, part of the rich eastern seaboard, and has a landscape laced with canals, lakes and rivers connecting with the Yangtze River.

Developers are hard put to keep up with the demand from potential homeowners for characterful luxury living. A piece of Dutch avant-garde design would certainly be an exotic species dropped down on this Chinese river plain. A blanket of tarmac dotted with natural and artificial features is to cover the oblong site. Holes cut into this coverlet make room for islands of garden houses, town houses, serpent-like or broken lines of terraces, star-shaped or square apartment towers, schools and a community centre. Amoeba and kidney shapes predominate with the insertion of gardens dedicated to roses, bamboo, fountains, raked and gargoyle stones, or hard sports courts for tennis and team ball games.

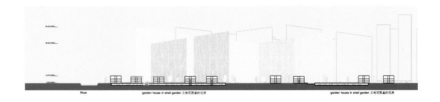

Buildings are integrated into the park as part of the island structures. The idea is to define a dense urban area by its greenery, soft and hard textures, rather than by grids of roads and circulation routes. Artfully designed hard landscaping can take the form of shells or glass fragments lit from below and sculptural eight metre high neon lights, not just cobbles. Over 50% of the site is green and the public realm is to be treated as a matrix of recreational open space for all ages, from kite flyers to Tai Chi exercisers, joggers to skaters and parents pushing baby buggies. Lines and words on the soft tarmac, for vehicle parking or as art installations of poetry verses, will be softened by the use of colour. Most parking, 85%, will be underground, beneath the housing or in covered mounds. At the site edges beside the river a beach atmosphere will be created and on the road boundaries multi-layered vegetation will form a buffer zone. Distributary roads, bike lanes and pedestrian ways within the site are convoluting and irregular to lower vehicle speeds and play a secondary role to landscaping.

For those who can afford this first class community living Phoenix City would offer all the features demanded by the emerging Chinese middle-class; privacy for the shrinking clans of one child families and singles but within an artificially created collective atmosphere, and the choice of a variety of individualized living spaces.

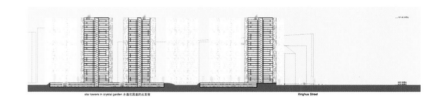

site section west - east to the south of Gangtian Road
俯-路东西向到南向的基地剖面 1:1000

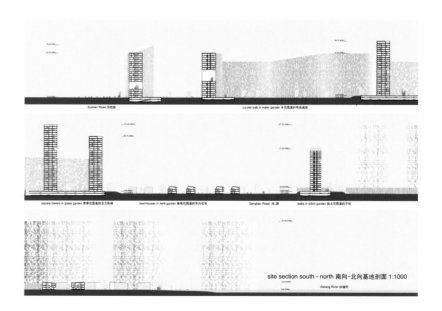

site section south - north 南向-北向基地剖面 1:1000

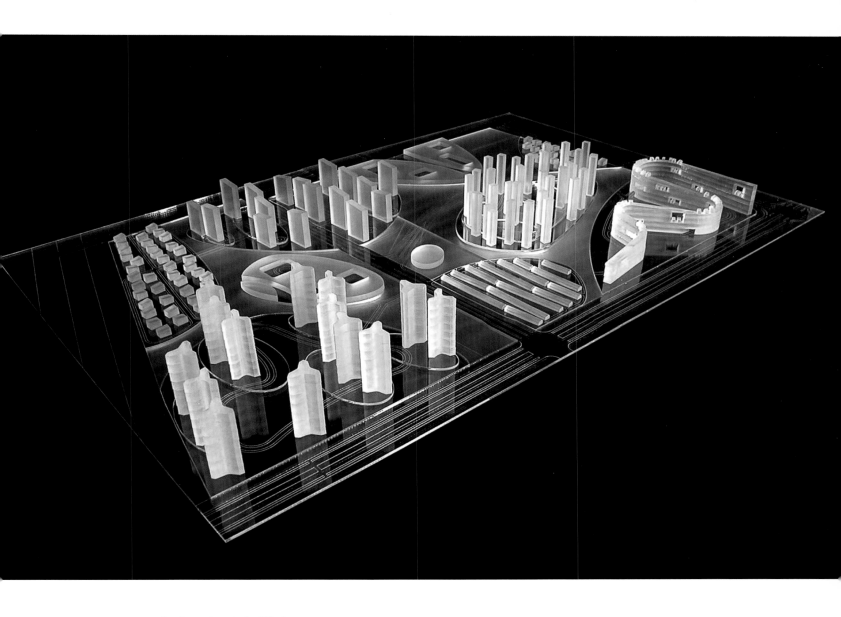

**Dutch avant-garde for China's new sandwich class suburbanites?**

tarmac riddled with natural and artificial elements as public surface
如同公共区域表面 铺满路胜表面铺满了自然及人工的材料充案

islands as gardens creating the immediate addresses
如同花园,岛屿创造了家的直接印象

volumes set according to shade and viewing principles
容积的设定是依据阴影及视觉原则

street network stimulating the use of public space
街道及环状系统的架构横式将会刺激及鼓励开放区域的使用率

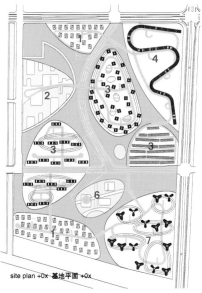

site plan +0x 基地平面 +0x

1 Garden houses

2 Public and private school

3 Square towers

4 Townhouses

5 Chamber

6 Community centre

7 Star towers

# LOOPED HYBRID, BEIJING

Completion 2006

The brief asked for an ultra-modern expression of twenty-first-century urban life for 2,500 inhabitants. Without an existing typographical context to play with the architect has invented his own setting on a 6.18 hectare site near Beijing's former city walls. In the ancient capital once riddled with enclaves for every class, from hovels to palaces, this is a modern, walled city with eight, irregularly-planned and placed towers linked by streets in the sky. These transparent clad bridges sit on top of over 700 apartments, shops, a multiplex of cinemas, nursery school, and underground car park and form a circular sky promenade of penthouse exhibition galleries, gym and jazz clubs, a library, and cafes. Privileged users look down on their city and the public peers up at the residents moving between their towers.

At the centre of this looped hybrid structure is an urban park. While the apartment clusters take on the mantle of China's rapidly disappearing fortified urban heritage the park is a post modern interpretation of Suzhou's meditative gardens or Hangzhou islands in the West Lake. Every artificial mound, created from site excavations, has been given a symbolic name; Mount of Childhood, Mount of Adolescence, Mount of Middle Age, Mount of Old Age and Mount of Infinity. Will residents, like ancient scholars, find these places an inspiration for painting, music and poetry? The park is public but the activity centres within the park are for residents only and electronically monitored to help keep them exclusive.

Light and colour is to be used to create mood, help orientation and indicate passing time. The underbellies of the bridges are brightly coloured as in classical Chinese architecture. Water movement activates night lights and cuts from movie images are projected on to the external walls of the cinema complex and surrounding water. The emphasis on a continually changing environment and unique spaces is not only a design concept but proclaimed as an ideological statement. This project design breaks with the past while remaining firmly rooted in the past.

Unlike other contemporary solitary towers this is a collective, another city within the city, with its own laundries and florists, but also sustainable and technologically advanced building systems. Prefabrication of the envelope, using computerised schedules, makes possible 'beamless' interiors with flat plate ceilings. Internal planning of the apartments does away with corridors and Feng-Shui is said to have been employed for harmonious orientation.

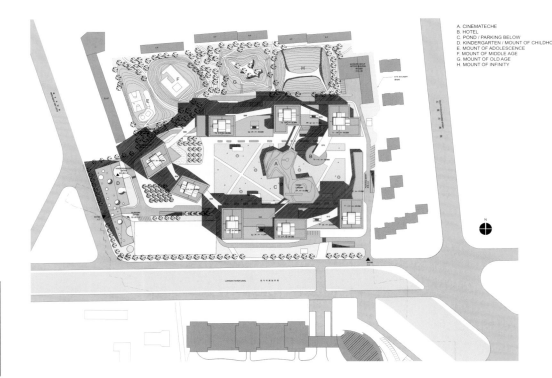

A. CINEMATECHE
B. HOTEL
C. POND / PARKING BELOW
D. KINDERGARTEN / MOUNT OF CHILDHOOD
E. MOUNT OF ADOLESCENCE
F. MOUNT OF MIDDLE AGE
G. MOUNT OF OLD AGE
H. MOUNT OF INFINITY

**An American Modernist's take on a Chinese classical walled city**

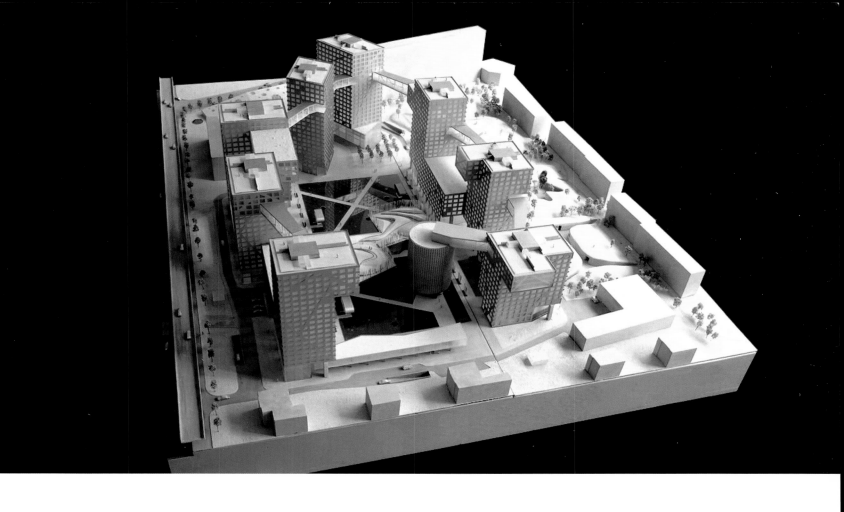

## Neighborhood 邻里格局

City of Dense Streets and Courtyards
密布街道和院落的城市

Traditional Neighborhoods
传统的邻里格局

City of Pockets Caused by New Residential Development and Uncoordinated privatization
口袋城市 由各自为政的私有化和新住宅开发造成

Alternative
其他选择

Alternative
其他选择

Alternative
其他选择

?

## Space 空间

Horizontality 水平

Beijing Before 1980s 80年代前的北京

Verticality 竖直

Beijing After 1980s 80年代后的北京

Proposed 建议

Vertical Horizontality 竖直的水平性

City of Objects 物体的城市

City of Spaces 空间的城市

## Open Community and Hybrid Programing 开放社区和混合功能

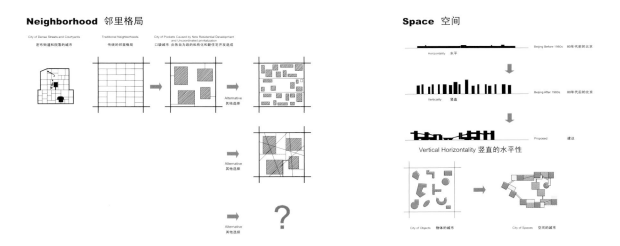

Average 191 m2

Education/Health
Culture/Sport
Commercial/Services
Bank/Post/Management

Panning 展租划

Sky Gardens 空中花园

Hybrid 混合

Apartments 153,000 m2
住宅 153,000平米

Required Service 11,100 m2
附属公建 11,100平米

Apartment

Service

Recreation

Service

Gardens

Apartment

Commercial

Gardens

Recreation

Apartment

Commercial

Upside Down 上下翻转

Hybrid 混合

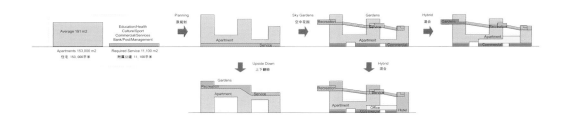

Gardens

Recreation

Apartment

Service

Recreation

Service

Apartment

Office

Commercial

Hotel

As a model it looks like an intricate obstacle course. But this chaos of pools, bridges, and a closed loop of apartment towers, might be a welcome antidote to the rigidly regimented developments in other new city districts.

# ARCHITECTS

**Paul Andreu architecte**  Paris, France
www.paul-andreu.com

**Wiel Arets Architect & Associates**  Maastricht,
The Netherlands
www.wielarets.nl

**Behnisch, Behnisch & Partner**  Stuttgart, Germany
www.behnisch.com

**Mario Botta Architetto**  Lugano, Switzerland
www.botta.ch

**Burckhardt + Partner**  Zurich, Switzerland
www.burckhardtpartner.ch

**Foster and Partners**  London, U.K.
www.fosterandpartners.com

**gmp von Gerkan, Marg und Partner**  Hamburg, Germany
www.gmp-architekten.de

**Zaha Hadid Architects**  London, U.K.
www.zaha-hadid.com

**Henn Architekten**  Munich, Germany
www.henn.com

**Steven Holl Architects**  New York, NY, U.S.A.
www.stevenholl.com

**Kohn Pedersen Fox Associates**  New York, NY, U.S.A.
www.kpf.com

**Dennis Lau & Ng Chun Man Architects**  Hong Kong, China
www.dln.com.hk

**MADA s.p.a.m.**  Shanghai, China
www.madaspam.com

**OMA Office for Metropoilitan Architecture**  Rotterdam,
The Netherlands
www.oma.nl

**Pei Partnership Architects**  New York, NY, U.S.A.
www.ppa-ny.com

**P&T Group**  Hong Kong, China
www.p-t-group.com

**Rocco Design**  Hong Kong, China
www.roccodesign.com

**RTKL Associates**  Baltimore, MD, U.S.A.
www.rtkl.com

**Sasaki Associates**  Boston, MA , U.S.A.
www.sasaki.com

**SOM Skidmore Owings & Merrill**  Chicago, IL, U.S.A.
www.som.com

**AS&P Albert Speer & Partner**  Frankfurt am Main,
Germany
www.as-p.de

# CLIENTS AND CONSULTANTS

## TOURISM · TRANSPORT

**Paul Andreu, Shanghai Pudong International Airport**

CLIENT  Shanghai Pudong International Airport
CONSULTANTS  Associate Architects: ADP/Architectes et
Ingenieurs | Structural Engineer: Coyne et Bellier | Building
Services: Setec | Lighting Consultant: Yann Kersale |
Landscape Architect: Michel Devisgne

**Foster and Partners, Beijing Capital International Airport Terminal 3**

CLIENT  Beijing Capital International Airport Co.
CONSULTANTS  Engineers: Ove Arup & Partners | Airport
Planners: NACO | Chinese Partners: Beijing Institute of
Architectural Design and Research

## MASTERPLANS

**Zaha Hadid with Patrik Schumacher, Soho City Masterplan, Beijing**

CLIENT  SOHO China, Beijing
CONSULTANTS  Urban Consultant: Ricky Burdett, London.

**Kohn Pedersen Fox Associates, Hua Mao Centre Masterplan, Beijing**

CLIENT  Guohua Real Estate Company
CONSULTANTS  Associate Architect: ECADI East China
Architectural Design Institute | Structural, Mechanical and
Electrical Engineers: BIAD 1st Design Studio, ECADI |
Cladding: ALT Cladding & Design Inc. | Lighting: Kugler
Tillotson Associates | Landscape Architects: EDAW

**AS&P Albert Speer & Partner, Central Axis Masterplan, Beijing**

CLIENT  Beijing Municipal Planning Commission
CONSULTANTS  Chinese Academy of Sciences, Beijing;
Research Centre for Eco-Environmental Sciences; Beijing
SunZhou Architectural Consulting | Landscape Architects:
WGF Werkgemeinschaft Freiraum, Nürnberg | Lighting
Concept: Kardorff Ingenieure, Berlin

**AS&P Albert Speer & Partner, Expo 2010 Masterplan, Shanghai**

CLIENT  Shanghai Urban Planning Administration Bureau

## STATE ORGANISATIONS

**Pei Partnership Architects, Bank of China Head Office, Beijing**

CLIENT  Beijing Bank of China Building Co. Ltd.
CONSULTANTS  Structural Engineers: Weidlinger Associates |
Mechanical Engineers: Jaros, Baum & Bolles | Design
Institute: China Academy of Building Research | Curtainwall &
Stonework: P. Y. Chin Architects | Interior Design: George C. T.
Woo & Partners | Lighting: Kugler Tillotson Associates |
Audio-Visual & Acoustics: Shen Milsom & Wilke | Quantity
Surveyor: Davis Langdon Seah | Communications, Information
Technology & PABX: Ove Arup & Partners, Hong Kong | Traffic:
Travers Associates | Specifications: Raymond Searby |
Graphics, Interior Signage: Tracy Turner Design Inc. | Stone
Inspection: Independent Stone Consulting | Trading Room:
Infact Consulting Pty. Ltd.

**OMA Office for Metropolitan Architecture, CCTV Central Chinese
Television Headquarters, Beijing**

CLIENT  China Central Television CCTV
CONSULTANTS  Associate Architects and Engineers: East
China Architecture & Design Institute (ECADI) | Structural and
Mechanical Engineers: Ove Arup & Partners, London and Hong
Kong | Strategic Advisor: Ma Qingyun, Shanghai | High Rise
Consultant: DMJMH + N, Los Angeles | Curtainwalling: Front,
New York | Broadcast Design: ECADI, Shanghai/Sandy Brown
Associates, London | Acoustics: Dorsser Blesgraaf, Eindhoven |
Scenography: DuckS Scéno, France | Vertical Transportation:
Lerch Bates & Associates, London | Lighting: LPA, Tokyo

**P&T Group, Police Headquarters, Shunde**

CLIENT  Government of Shunde
CONSULTANTS  P&T Group Architects and Engineers Ltd.

**Kohn Pedersen Fox Associates, China Natural Offshore Oil
Corporation Headquarters, Beijing**

CLIENT  China Natural Offshore Oil Corporation
CONSULTANTS  Structural, Mechanical, Electrical and
Plumbing Engineers: China Architecture Design & Research
Group, Beijing | Wall cladding and Building Maintenance:
Meinhardt Façade Technologies, Melbourne | Landscape
Architects and Fountain Design: JingHua Landscape Design and
Engineering Office – Beijing Botanical Gardens | Interior
Lighting: Brandston Partnership, New York | Exterior Lighting:
Lighting & Sound Engineering Research Corp., Beijing

**Henn Architekten, China Petro Headquarters, Beijing**

CLIENT  China Petro, Beijing

**Dennis Lau & Ng Chun Man, Citic Plaza, Tien Ho, Guangzhou**

CLIENT  China International Trust & Investment Corporation
CONSULTANTS  Dennis Lau & Ng Chun Man Architects & Engineers (HK) Ltd.

## CORPORATE · FINANCIAL · MIXED COMPLEXES

**Foster and Partners, Jiushi Corporation Headquarters, Shanghai**

CLIENT  Jiushi Corporation
CONSULTANTS  Designers: Obayashi Corporation design Department | Chinese Partners: East China Architectural Design Institute (ECADI) | Lighting Design: Claude R. Engle Lighting

**Kohn Pedersen Fox Associates, World Financial Centre, Shanghai**

CLIENT  Forest Overseas Co. Ltd.
CONSULTANTS  Structural Engineers: Leslie Robertson Associates R.L.L.P. | Executive Architects: Irie Miyake Architects and Engineers | Project Architects: Mori Building Company Ltd. | Wallcladding: ALT Cladding & Design | Landscape Architects: Hargreaves and Associates

**MADA s.p.a.m., Shopping Maze, Central Business District, Wuxi S.E.Z.**

CLIENT  Wuxi City Investment Co. Ltd.
CONSULTANTS  Partner: Wuxi Architecture Institute

**MADA s.p.a.m., Y-Town, Central Commercial District and Cultural Centre, Ningbo**

CLIENT  Ningbo City Investment Co. Ltd. | apartment Co. Ltd., Japan
CONSULTANTS  China State Construction Engineering Co. | Shanghai Architecture Institute | Lets Co. Ltd.

**Kohn Pedersen Fox Associates, Plaza 66, Nanjing Xi Lu, Shanghai**

CLIENT  Hang Lung Development Co. Ltd.
CONSULTANTS PHASE I  Associated Architects: Frank C.Y. Feng Architects and Associates (HK) Ltd. | Structural Engineers: Thornton Tomasetti Engineers | Mechanical, Electrical and Plumbing Engineers: Flack & Kurtz Consulting Engineers | Lighting: Kugler Tillotson Associates | Vertical Transportation: John A. Van Deusen & Associates Inc. | Retail Consultants: D.I. Design
CONSULTANTS PHASE II  Local Architects: LM2 Consortium SDN. BHD. | Structural Engineers: Thornton Tomasetti Engineers | Mechanical, Electrical and Plumbing Engineers: Associated Consulting Engineers Ltd. | Vertical Transportation: Lerch, Bates & Associates Inc. | Wind Tunnel Consultants: Rowan Williams Davis & Irwin Inc. | Quantity Surveyors: Davis Langdon & Seah

**Dennis Lau & Ng Chun Mann, Jinguanghua Retail Complex, Renmin Lu, Shenzhen**

CLIENT  Shenzhen Jinguanghua Group
CONSULTANTS  Dennis Lau & Ng Chun Man Architects & Engineers (HK) Ltd.

## TRADE · CONVENTIONS · EXHIBITIONS

**gmp von Gerkan, Marg und Partner, Convention and Exhibition Centre (SZCEC), Shenzhen**

CLIENT  Shenzhen Convention & Exhibition Centre
CONSULTANTS  Chinese Partner: China Northeast Architectural Design Institute, Shenzhen | Structural Engineer: Schlaich Bergermann und Partner | Building Services: HL-Technik

**SOM Skidmore Owings & Merrill, International Expo Centre, Suzhou**

CLIENT  Suzhou International Expo Center Co., Ltd.
CONSULTANTS  Partner: Beijing Institute of Architectural Design and Research | Landscape: SWA | Lighting: PHA | Fire Precautions: Rolf Jensen & Associates Inc.

**Henn Architekten, International Automotive Expo, Beijing**

CLIENT  Construction Office of Beijing, International Vehicle Expo Center
CONSULTANTS  Partner Architect: B+ H Architects, Shanghai

## SCIENCE · TECHNOLOGY · LEARNING

**Kohn Pedersen Fox Associates, Zhongguancun West, BSTP Lot 21, Haidian, Beijing**

CLIENT  Beijing Science & Technology Park
CONSULTANTS  Associate Architect: China Architectural Research Design Institute | Structural, Mechanical and Electrical Engineers: Meinhardt Ltd. | Curtainwalling: ALT Cladding & Design Inc. | Lighting: Kugler Tillotson Associates

**RTKL Associates, Museum of Science and Technology, Pudong, Shanghai**

CLIENT  Shanghai Science Land Development Co., Ltd.
CONSULTANTS  Associate Architects: Shanghai Modern Design Group | Structural Engineer: Ove Arup & Partners, LA, USA | Museum Exhibit Consultant: DMCD Incorporated, New York, USA

**Dennis Lau & Ng Chun Man, Hua Wei Technologies Headquarters and International Training Centre, Buji Bantian, Long Gang District, Shenzhen**

CLIENT  Hua Wei Technologies Co. Ltd.
CONSULTANTS  Dennis Lau & Ng Chun Man Architects & Engineers (HK) Ltd.

**MADA s.p.a.m., Zhejiang University Library, Ningbo Campus, Zhejiang**

CLIENT  Zhejiang University
CONSULTANTS  Zhejiang Architecture and Research Institute

**gmp von Gerkan, Marg und Partner, German School and Apartments, Beijing**

CLIENT  Federal Republic of Germany
CONSULTANTS  Structural Engineer: Weber-Poll Ingenieure | Construction: Philipp Holzmann

Rocco Design, Guangzhou Library, Zhujiang New Town, Guangzhou's New City Centre

CLIENT Guangzhou Municipal Development Planning Commission
CONSULTANTS Guangzhou Urban Planning & Design Survey Research Institute

## CULTURE

Paul Andreu, National Theatre, Chang An Avenue, Beijing

CLIENT The National Grand Theatre Committee
CONSULTANTS Associate Architects: ADPi | Collaborating Consultants: BIAD | Engineering: Setec

Paul Andreu, Oriental Art Centre, Century Avenue, Pudong, Shanghai

CLIENT Shanghai Pudong New Area Culture Broadcast Television Bureau
CONSULTANTS Associate Architects: ADPi | Collaborating Consultant: ECADI | Structural Engineer: Coyne et Bellier | Façade Engineer: R. Peltier | Scenography: BSEDI | Acoustics Consultant: CSTB and Xu Acoustique

Zaha Hadid Architects, Guangzhou Opera House, Guangzhou, Guangdong Province

CLIENT Guangzhou Municipal Government

Pei Partnership Architects, Art Museum, Suzhou

CLIENT City of Suzhou, Suzhou Municipal Administration of Culture, Radio & Television
CONSULTANTS Design Institute: Suzhou Institute of Architectural Design Co. Ltd. | Structural Engineers: Leslie E. Robertson Associates, R.L.L.P., New York | Mechanical and Electrical Engineers: Jaros Baum & Bolles, New York | Lighting: Fisher Marantz Stone & Partners | Exhibition design Consultant: James C.Y. Watt | Acoustics: Albert Xu, Xu-Acoustique

Rocco Design, Guangdong Museum, Zhujiang New Town, Guangzhou's New City Centre

CLIENT Guangzhou Municipal Government
CONSULTANTS Structural Engineers: Ove Arup & Partners Hong Kong Ltd. | Building Services: Meinhardt (M&E) ltd. | Lighting: Tokyo Shomei Consultant | Local Consultants: Guangdong Architectural Design Institute

RTKL Associates, Chinese Museum of Film, Beijing

CLIENT China Film Museum Project Committee, Beijing Radio, Film and Television Bureau
CONSULTANTS Collaborating Consultants: Beijing Institute of Architecture Design and Research | Structural Engineers: Wong Hobach Lau, International, Los Angeles, USA | Lighting: Illuminating Concepts, Michigan, USA | Cinema Consultants: STK Architecture Inc., California, USA | Fire Consultants: Rolf Jensen & Associates, USA

gmp von Gerkan, Marg und Partner, National Museum, Tiananmen Square, Beijing

CLIENT The National Museum of China

gmp von Gerkan, Marg und Partner, Museum Archives and Exhibition Hall for Urban Development, Pudong, Shanghai

CLIENT City of Shanghai, New District Pudong
CONSULTANTS Chinese Partner: Shanghai Institute of Architectural Design & Research Co., Ltd.

Mario Botta, Museum and Art Gallery, Tsinghua University, Beijing

CLIENT Tsinghua University, Beijing
CONSULTANTS Architect of Record and Engineers: China Academy of Building Research, Beijing

P&T Group, Culture Complex, Shunde New City

CLIENT Government of Shunde
CONSULTANTS P&T Group Architects and Engineers Ltd.

AS&P Albert Speer & Partner, Interconfessional Prayer Hall, Zhang Jiang Hi-Tech Park, Pudong, Shanghai

CLIENT Zhang Jiang Hi-Tech Park Corporation

## SPORT

Paul Andreu, Guangzhou Gymnasium, Guangzhou

CLIENT Guangzhou Municipal Government
CONSULTANTS Associates: ADPi | Collaborating Consultant: Guangzhou Design Institute | Structural Engineer: Aéroports de Paris | Equipment Design: Setec

Sasaki Associates Inc., Olympic Green, Beijing

CLIENT Beijing Olympic Games Organising Committee

Herzog & de Meuron, National 2008 Olympic Stadium, Beijing

CLIENT Beijing People's Government | Organizer: Beijing Municipal Planning Commission | Competition Authority: Beijing Municipal Government, Beijing Organising Committee for the Games of the XXIX Olympiad (BOCGO)
CONSULTANTS Artist: Ai Weiwei | Design Institute: China Architecture Design and Research Group, Beijing | Structural Engineers, Transport Planners, Sustainability and Acoustics Consultants: Arup Sports, Manchester | Quantity Surveyors: Davis Langdon & Everest, London

Burckhardt + Partner, 2008 Olympics Wukesong Cultural and Sports Center, Beijing

CONSULTANTS Engineers: Lüchinger + Meyer Bauingenieure AG | Communications: Communications Consultants Comfa AG | Acoustics: ADA Acoustic Design Ahnert | Traffic/Spatial Planners: Ernst Basler + Partner AG | Building Services: Building Technique HL-Technik AG | Fire Protection: Air Flow Consulting | Project Management: Karl Steiner AG

## NEW TOWNS AND HOMES

**AS&P Albert Speer & Partner, Anting International Automobile City and New Town, Anting, Shanghai**

CLIENT  Shanghai Urban Planning Administration Bureau of the Shanghai Jia Ding District  |  Shanghai International Autocity Real Estate Development Co. Ltd.

**Behnisch, Behnisch & Partner, Anting New Town Neighbourhood, Anting, Shanghai**

CLIENT  Shanghai International Automobile City Real Estate Co.

**gmp von Gerkan, Marg und Partner, Luchao Harbour City, Shanghai**

CLIENT  Shanghai Urban Planning Administration Bureau
CONSULTANTS  Port Planning: HPC Hamburg Port Consulting  |  Landscape Architect: Breimann, Bruun  |  Light Planning: Schlotfeldt Licht

**Rocco Design with Iroje Architect, Boao Canal Village, Hainan Island**

CLIENT  Private Developer
CONSULTANTS  Masterplan: Rocco Design Ltd.  |  Partner Architect: Iroje Architect  |  Civil and Geotechnical Engineers: Ove Arup & Partners  |  Structural Engineers: Beijing Architectural Design Institute of China State Construction Engineering Corp.

**Wiel Arets Architect & Associates, Phoenix City, Suzhou**

CLIENT  Shanghai Sunco Group Co.

**Steven Holl Architects, Looped Hybrid, Beijing**

CLIENT  Modern Hongyun Real Estate Development Co. Ltd., Beijing
CONSULTANTS  Associate Architect: Beijing Capital Engineering Architecture Design Co., Ltd.  |  Structural Engineer: Guy Nordenson and Associates  |  Mechanical Engineer: TRANSSOLAR Energietechnik GmbH, consentini Associates  |  Consulting Engineer: China Academy of Building Research  |  Lighting Designer: Halie Light and L'Observatoire International

# PLACE NAMES

The three Roman spelling systems for Chinese place names are:
the Colonial Post-Office Form, the Wade Giles System and Modern Pinyin

| | | | | | |
|---|---|---|---|---|---|
| Amoy | Hsia-men | Xiamen | Ningpo | Ning-po | Ningbo |
| Anhwei Province | An-hui | Anhui | Pagoda Island | *n/a* | Luoxing |
| Canton | Kuang-chou | Guangzhou | Pakhoi | Pei-hai | Beihai |
| Changsha | Ch'ang-sha | Changsha | Peking | Pei-ching | Beijing |
| Chefoo | n/a | Yantai | Port Arthur | Lu-shun | Lushun |
| Chekiang Province | n/a | Zhejiang | Sanmen Bay | San-men wan | Sanmen wan |
| Chengtu | Ch'eng-tu | Chengdu | Shameen | Sha-mien | Shamian |
| Chihli Province | Chih-li | Zhili | Shanghai | Shang-hai | Shanghai |
| Chinkiang | Chin-chiang | Zhenjiang | Shansi Province | Shan-hsi | Shanxi |
| Chungking | Ch'ung-ch'ing | Chongqing | Shantung Province | Shan-tung | Shandong |
| Chusan archipelago | Chou-shan tao | Zhoushan dao | Shasi | Sha-ssu | Shasi |
| Dairen | Ta-lien | Luda (Dalian) | Shensi Province | Shan-hsi | Shaanxi |
| Foochow | Fu-chou | Fuzhou | Sian | Hsi-an | Xi'an |
| Fukien Province | Fu-chien | Fujian | Sinkiang Province | Hsin-chiang | Xinjiang |
| Fushan | Fu-shan | Fushan | Soochow | Su-chou | Suzhou |
| Hainan | Hai-nan | Hainan | Swatow | Shan-t'ou | Shantou |
| Hangchow | Hang-chou | Hangzhou | Szechwan Province | Ssu-ch'uan | Sichuan |
| Hankow | Han-k'ou | Hankou (Wuhan) | Taiwan | T'ai-wan | Taiwan |
| Hanyang | Han-yang | Hanyang | Tientsin | T'ien-chin | Tianjin |
| Harbin | Ha-erh-pin | Haerbin | Tsingtao | Ts'ing-tao | Qingdao |
| Honan Province | He-nan | Henan | Wanghsia | Wang-hsia | Wangxia |
| Hongkew | Hung-ch'iu | Hongqu | Weihaiwei | Wei-hai-wei | Weihaiwei |
| Hong Kong | n/a | Xianggang | Whampoa | Huang-p'u | Huangpu |
| Hsuchow | Hsu-chou | Xuzhou | Woosong | Wu-sung | Wusong |
| Kansu Province | Kan-su | Gansu | Wuchang | Wu-ch'ang | Wuchang |
| Kiangsi Province | Chiang-hsi | Jiangxi | Wuchow | Wu-chou | Wuzhou |
| Kiangsu Province | Chiang-su | Jiangsu | Wuhan | Wu-han | Wuhan |
| Kiaochow Bay | Ch'iao-chou wan | Jiaozhou Wan | Wuhsi | Wu-hsi | Wuxi |
| Kuangchow Bay | Kuang-chou wan | Guangzhou wan | Wuhu | Wu-hu | Wuhu |
| Kunming | K'un-ming | Kunming | Yangchow | Yang-chou | Yangzhou |
| Kwangsi Province | Kuang-hsi | Guangxi | Yunnan Province | Yun-nan | Yunnan |
| Kweichow Province | Kuei-chou | Guizhou | | | |
| Liaoyung | Liao-tung | Liaodong | | | |
| Lintin Island | Ling-ting | Lingding | | | |
| Lungchow | Lung-chou | Longzhou | | | |
| Lushan | Lu-shan | Lushan | | | |
| Macao | Ao-men | Aomen | | | |
| Nanchang | Nan-ch'ang | Nanchang | | | |
| Nanking | Nan-ching | Nanjing | | | |
| Nanning | Nan-ning | Nanning | | | |
| Newchwang | Ying-k'ou | Yingkou | | | |

# A CHRONOLOGY OF DYNASTIES
# AND HISTORIC LANDMARK EVENTS

**2070–1600 B.C.**
Xia

**1600–1046 B.C.**
Shang **B.C.**

**1046–771 B.C.**
Western Zhou

**770–476 B.C.**
Eastern Zhou, Spring and Autumn period

**475–221 B.C.**
Eastern Zhou, Warring States period

**221–207 B.C.**
Qin dynasty—beginning of unification and expansion

**206–24 A.D.**
Western Han

**25–220**
Eastern Han

**220–265**
Three Kingdoms

**265–316**
Western Jin

**317–420**
Eastern Jin

**420–589**
Southern and Northern Dynasties

**581–618**
Sui

**618–907**
Tang

**907–960**
Five Dynasties

**960–1127**
Northern Song

**1127–1279**
Southern Song

**1271–1368**
Yuan

**1368–1644**
Ming

**1644–1911**
Qing Manchu dynasty

**1839**
First Opium War. Chinese capture and destroy foreign imports of opium. British ships fire on Chinese junks in Canton.

**1841**
Britain declares Hong Kong part of British Empire.

**1842**
Treaty of Nanking ends First Opium War, hands over to Queen Victoria and her descendants the island of Hong Kong in perpetuity, and opens Shanghai, Ningpo, Foochow, Amoy and Canton to foreign trade.

**1845**
There follows the Sino-American Treaty of Wanghsia in Macao and the Sino-French Treaty of Whampoa, which extends privileges for the British in the Treaty of Nanking to the Americans and French. Up until this date it had been illegal for foreigners to learn Chinese, or for Chinese to teach them.

**1856**
Second Opium War.

British crew of 'The Arrow' arrested by the Viceroy of Canton on suspicion of piracy. British warships fire on Canton.

**1860**
Sino-British and Sino-French Treaties of Tientsin and Conventions of Peking, signed by British, French, Americans and Russians, end the second Opium War, allowing foreign ambassadors to live in Peking, opening up more cities for foreign trade and residence, especially along the Yangtze and in the interior.

**1861**
Hankow, Chinkiang, Kiukiang on the Yangtze, Swatow, Taiwan, Pagoda Island and Hoihow in the south and Chefoo and Newchwang in the north are opened as treaty ports.

**1863**
In Shanghai British and American concessions are merged to form the International Settlement, a Mixed Court for dealing with foreigners is set up, Shanghai Club is founded, and Sir Robert Hart becomes Inspector-General of the Chinese Imperial Maritime Customs.

**1865**
First western-style arsenal built just outside Shanghai by Tseng Kuo-fan to produce western weapons.

**1866**
Western shipyard built in Foochow.

**1870**
London and Shanghai connected by undersea electric cable.

**1876**
Chefoo Agreement opens Ichang and Wuhu on the Yangtze and Wenchow and Pakhoi to trade.

**1878**
First western Shanghai cotton mill set up.

**1881**
In Shanghai concessions telephone system and water company established. Shanghai and Tientsin joined by telegraph.

**1885**
In Shanghai, the British missionary John Fryer and the Chinese founded Shanghai Polytechnic to teach Chinese modern science and technology.

**1890**
Additional Article to Chefoo Agreement opens Chungking to trade.

**1895**
As a result of the Sino-Japanese war the Japanese are allowed to trade and live in China. Ssumao in Yunnan becomes a treaty port.

**1896**
First film shown in Shanghai. Tientsin-Peking railway built.

**1897**
After the German Minister in China demands a fifty-year lease on Kiaochow Bay, in Shantung, Germans seize the Bay by force. Russian warships enter Port Arthur under pretence of protecting China from Germany.

Shasi, Samshui, Soochow and Hangchow become treaty ports following the Sino-Japanese War.

**1898**
Russia is granted a twenty-five-year lease on Port Arthur and Dairen. Germany is granted Kiaochow Bay. Britain gets a lease on Weihaiwei.

**1899**
Railway concessions ceded to Russia and Germany. France gains a ninety-nine-year lease on Kuangchow Bay. Yochow in Hunan becomes a Treaty Port.

**1901**
Following Boxer rebels' massacre of foreigners, The Boxer Protocol, signed by Germany, Britain, Austria, Belgium, Spain, USA, France, Italy, Holland and Russia, requires China to pay huge indemnity.

**1902**
Cars imported into Shanghai.

**1904**
Russo-Japanese War fought in China.

**1908**
First trams in Shanghai.

**1911**
Nanking becomes the national capital after the Qing imperial house is overthrown.

**1911**
The Republic of China founded with Sun Yat-sen as first president.

**1919**
Paris Peace Conference at end of the World War I gives Japan former German territories in China.

**1921**
First Communist Party congress in the French Concession of Shanghai.

**1921–39**
Civil War among war lords, bandits, Nationalists and Communists. Chinese workers strike against foreign industrialists, the last emperor (Puyi) leaves the Forbidden City.

On Sun Yat-sen's death Chiang Kai-shek becomes the leader of the Nationalists and their capital is Hangkow. The Japanese invade China and set Puyi up as their puppet Chinese Emperor.

**1939–45**
World War II in Europe. After 1941, the war extends to the Pacific. Thousands of Jewish European refugees arrive in Shanghai. Japan controls Chinese Treaty Ports and foreigners are interned.

**1943**
Britain and USA return all territorial rights, on the mainland, to the Chinese.

**1949**
The People's Republic of China declared by Mao.

**1978**
Open Door Policies and Four Modernisations formulated by Deng Xiaoping.

**1980**
SEZ Special Economic Zones designated: Shenzhen, Zhuhai, Shantou, Xiamen.

**1985**
100 'Open' Chinese cities.

**1988**
288 'Open' Chinese cities.

**1997**
Hong Kong returns to China.

**1999**
Macau returns to China.

**2001**
China becomes WTO member.

**2008**
Beijing to host Olympics.

**2010**
Shanghai to host World Expo.

# BIBLIOGRAPHY

Listed in chronological order

*Inside the New China*, Fortune, European Edition Special Issue 10/2004

Tony Saich, *Governance and Politics of China*, Palgrave Macmillan, London 2004

Rocco Yim, *Being Chinese in Architecture*, MCCM Creations, 2004

*China 2004*, Verlag Neuer Stern, Beijing 2004

Carl Fingerhuth, *Learning from China: Das Tao der Stadt*, Birkhäuser Verlag, Basel 2004

'Chinesischer Hochgeschwindigkeitsurbanismus', Theme Issue: 168 Archplus, Zeitschrift für Architektur und Städtebau, Aachen 02/2004

MADA s.p.a.m., *On Site*, Aedes, Berlin 2004

*Shanghai Urban Planning*, Shanghai Urban Planning Administration Bureau, Shanghai 2004

Luigi Novelli, *Shanghai Architecture Guide*, Haiwen Audio-Video Publishers, Shanghai 2004

Luigi Novelli, *Shanghai Residential Buildings*, Haiwen Audio-Video Publishers, Shanghai 2003

*Alors, La Chine?*, exhib. cat., Centre Pompidou, Paris 2003

'Architecture in China', A&U Special Issue no. 12 (399), Tokyo 2003

Chu Zhi Hao, *Die moderne Chinesische Architektur im Spannungsfeld zwischen eigener Tradition und fremden Kulturen, Shanghai*, Lang, Frankfurt am Main 2003

*Yung Ho Chang: Atelier Feichang Jianzhu, A Chinese Practice*, Gutierrez + Portefaix, Map Book Publishers, Hong Kong 2003

*Ningpo: Metamorphosis of a Chinese City*, Aedes, Berlin 2003

Eduard Kögel, *Tangshan Xiangdeli: Neue Stadt in China*, jovis Verlag, Berlin 2003

von Gerkan Marg and Partner, *Luchao: Aus einem Tropfen geboren/Born from a Drop*, DZA Verlag, Altenburg 2003

Peter G. Rowe, Seng Kuan, *Architectural Encounters with Essence and Form in Modern China*, Cambridge, Mass., MIT Press, London 2002

John R. Logan, *The New Chinese City. Globalisation and Market Reform*, Blackwell Publishers, Oxford 2002

Yung Ho Chang, *21 Works of Atelier Feichang Jianzhu 1996–2001*, 2002

Alan Balfour, Zheng Shiling, *World Cities: Shanghai*, Wiley Academy, Chichester 2002

*Dennis Lau & NG Chun Man*, Mulgrave Images, 2002

*Shanghai Reflections: Architecture, Urbanism and the Search for an Alternative Modernity*, with essays by Mario Gandelsonas, Ackbar Abbas, M. Christine Boyer, Princeton Architectural Press, New York 2002

Almut E. I. Bettels, Li Yuxiang, *Traditional Architecture in China*, Benteli, Wabern 2002

Quinghua Guo, *A Visual Dictionary of Chinese Architecture*, Mulgrave Images, 2002

Carl Fingerhuth, Ernst Joos, *The Kunming Project: Urban Development in China—A Dialogue*, Birkhäuser, Basle 2002

Annping Chin, Jonathan Spence, *The Chinese Century*, Orion, London 2002

Nancy N. Chen, Constance D. Clark, Suzanne Z. Gottschang, Lyn Jeffery, *China Urban Ethnographies of Contemporary Culture*, Durham, London 2001

'Dongzhimen, Intertransport-Station Peking', (workshop) 09–10/ 2000, Hochschule für Bildende Künste Hamburg, 02/2001

*Tu Mu: Junge Architektur aus China/Young Architecture of China: Ai Wei Wei, Atelier Feichang Jianzhu, Liu Jiakun, MRMADA, Wang Shu, Nanda Jianzhu*, Aedes, Berlin, 2001

Michael Wolf, Harald Maass, *China im Wandel*, Frederking & Thaler, Munich 2001

Lu Junhua, P.G. Rowe, Zhang Jie, *Modern Urban Housing in China 1840–2000*, Prestel Verlag, Munich/Berlin/London/ New York 2001

Chuihua Judy Chung, Jeffrey Inaba, Rem Koolhaas, Sze Tsung Leong, *Great Leap Forward. Harvard Project on the City*, Taschen, Cologne 2001

E. Kögel, U. Meyer, *Die Chinesische Stadt: Zwischen Tradition und Moderne*, jovis Verlag, Berlin 2000

K. Vöckler, D. Luckow, *Beijing, Shanghai, Shenzhen: Städte des 21. Jahrhunderts/Cities of the 21st Century*, Campus Verlag, Frankfurt am Main 2000

Kai Vöckler, Dirk Luckow, *Peking, Shanghai, Schenzhen*, Campus Verlag, Frankfurt am Main 2000

Yinong Xu, *The Chinese City in Space and Time*, University of Hawaii Press, Honolulu 2000

Ronald Knapp, *China's Old Dwellings*, University of Hawaii Press, Honolulu 2000

Liangyong Wu, *Rehabilitating the Old City of Beijing. A Project in the Ju'er Hutong Neighbourhood*, University of Washington Press, Vancouver 1999

J. Zhu, S. Sassen, A.C. Coombes, et al., *Instant China: Notas sobre una transformación urbana/Notes on an urban transformation*, Nexus, Barcelona 1999

Luigi Novelli, *Shanghai: Architettura & Citta tra Cina e Occidente/Architecture & City between China and the West*, Edizioni Librerie Dedalo, Rome 1999

Valerie Steele, John S. Major, *China Chic—East Meets West*, Yale University Press, New Haven/London 1999

Ronald Knapp, *China's Living Houses*, University of Hawaii Press, Honolulu 1999

Frances Wood, *No Dogs and Not Many Chinese: Treaty Port Life in China 1843–1943*, John Murray Publishers, London 1998

'Suzhou: Shaping an Ancient City for the New China', (EDAW/ I.M. Pei workshop), with an epilogue by I.M. Pei, Spacemaker Press, Washington, Cambridge, Mass. 1998

*P&T Group: 130 Years of Architecture in Asia*, Pace Publishing Ltd., Hong Kong 1998

Hinz, Lind, *Tsingtau: Ein Kapitel deutscher Kolonialgeschichte in China 1897–1914*, Minerva, Eurasburg 1998

Torsten Warner, *German Architecture in China: Architectural Transfer*, Ernst & Sohn, Berlin 1994

Robert Kaltenbrunner, *Minhang, Shanghai. Die Satellitenstadt als Intermediäre Planung*, Technische Universität Berlin, Berlin 1993

Ronald Knapp, *The Chinese House: Craft, Symbol and the Folk Tradition*, Oxford University Press, Hong Kong 1990

Alfred Schinz, *Cities in China*, Lubrecht & Cramer Ltd., Berlin 1989

Victor Sit, *Chinese Cities: The Growth of the Metropolis since 1949*, Oxford University Press, Oxford 1988

Kerrie L. MacPherson, *A Wilderness of Marshes: The Origins of the Public Health in Shanghai 1843–1893*, Oxford University Press, Hong Kong 1987

Geremie Barmé, John Minford (eds.), *Seeds of Fire*, Far East Economic Review, 1986

Deng Pufang, 'Humanism for the Handicapped', in: China News Analysis, 1985

Sun Longji, *The Deep Structure of Chinese Culture*, Hong Kong 1983

*History Around Us: Preserving our Historic Buildings*, Hong Kong Museum of History, Urban Council, Hong Kong 1982

Wang Ruoshui, *In Defence of Socialist Humanism* (articles by the editor of 'Peoples Daily' 1950–83), 1983

Jin Guantao, *Behind the Phenomena of History* (collection of essays on Chinese feudalism), 12/1983

David Bonavia, *The Chinese: A Portrait*, Pelican Books, London 1982

Thomas Thilo, *Klassische Chinesische Baukunst: Strukturprinzipien und Soziale Funktion*, Tusch, Vienna 1977

*New China Builds*, ed. by the Academy of Building Research and the State Capital Construction Commission, China Building Industry Press, Peking 1976

Charles M. Dyce, *Personal Reminiscences of Thirty Years Residence in the Model Settlement Shanghai 1870–1900*, Chapman & Hall, London 1906

**Background Biographical and Documentary Literature:**

Chun Sue, *Beijing Doll*, Riverhead Books/Penguin/Abacus, London 2004

Sid Smith, *A House by the River*, Picador/Pan Macmillan, London 2003

Qiu Xiaolong, *A Loyal Character Dancer*, Soho Press, New York 2002

Gao Xingjian, *One Man's Bible*, Flamingo, London 2002

Dai Sijie, *Balzac and the Little Chinese Seamstress*, Chatto & Windus, London 2001

Ha Jin, *In the Pond*, Vintage/Random House, London 2001

*China after Mao* (photographs: Liu Heung Shing; introduction: Tiziano Terzani), Asia 2000 Ltd., Hong Kong 1987

Suyin Han, *Wind in the Tower, Mao Tsetung and the Chinese Revolution 1949–1975*, Triad Books, 1978

Suyin Han, *The Crippled Tree*, Triad Books, 1972

Suyin Han, *A Mortal Flower*, Triad Books, 1972

Suyin Han, *Birdless Summer*, Triad Books, 1972

Suyin Han, *My House has Two Doors*, Putnam Pub. Group, 1980

Suyin Han, *My House has Two Doors: Phoenix Harvest*, vol. 2, Grafton Books, 1982

Arthur Miller, *"Salesman" in Peking*, Methuen, London 1984

Mao Tun, *Midnight*, Peoples Literature Publishing House, Peking 1955

K.M. Gadd, Jack Chen, *Wang Shu Min*, Ginn and Company, London 1950

W.H. Auden, Christopher Isherwood, *Journey to a War* (first published in 1939), Faber and Faber, London 2002

# INDEX OF NAMES AND PLACES

## BUILDINGS AND PLACES

# ACKNOWLEDGEMENTS

# PICTURE CREDITS

Although this is a personal critique of China's architectural culture, many people around the world have given me practical support, hospitality and the benefit of their experience.

I am especially indebted to Christoph Krämer for composing a selection of his documentary photographs for the essay, Sayaid and Diana Shah, Professor Zheng Shiling, Vice President of The Architectural Society of China, President of The Architectural Society of Shanghai and Director of the Institute of Architecture & Urban Space at Tongji University, Liu Wei, Associate Professor at the Department of International Cultural Studies at Hangzhou's Zhejiang University and national television documentary maker, the architect Ann Mu at MADA s.p.a.m. in Shanghai, Remo Riva, Director of the P&T Group in S.E Asia, Rocco Yim of Rocco Design in Hong Kong, George Lam, Publisher at Pace Publishing in China, Neil and Anna McLaughlin of McLaughlin Projects in HK/Thailand, my many colleagues from my China years, and the international architects who generously provided information over the last three years.

Numbers refer to pages
(t top, b bottom, l left, c centre, r right)

Paul Andreu  38 b, 118, 149 b
ADPi  122, 123 b
Wiel Arets Architect & Associates  172, 173
AS&P Albert Speer & Partner  48, 49, 50, 51, 146, 147, 158, 159
AXYZ  119 b, 123 t
Behnisch, Behnisch & Partner  160–163
Mario Botta Architetto  142, 143
Buonomo/Langlais  120, 121
Burckhardt + Partner Architekten Zurich  10–11, 154–157
Crystal  46 b l, 47
Crystal Digital Technology Co. Ltd.  126 t, 127 t, b r
Crystal/Yuanjing/Dream Pix  100, 101
B. Dragon  119 t
H.G. Esch  84, 86, 87
Foster and Partners  4–5, 40–43, 71
Andreas Gärtner  91 t, 141 b
gmp von Gerkan, Marg und Partner  91 c, b, 110, 141 t, 164 t r, 166, 167
Tim Griffith  102–105
Zaha Hadid Architects  44, 45, 124, 125
Steven Holl Architects  176–179
Henn Architekten  6–7, 66–67, 96–99
Kiyohiko Higashide  52–55
Tian Pao Huang  36–37, 38 t
Kerun Ip  70–71, 72, 73
Kohn Pedersen Fox Associates  62 b r, 65 b, 74–77, 85
Christoph Krämer, Hamburg  16–33
Dennis Lau & Ng Chun Man  68, 69, 88, 89, 106, 107
Heiner Leiska  140, 164–165
Zhou Li/Point Studio  37
MADA s.p.a.m.  78–83, 108, 109
Paul Maurer  39
Micro Models/Xin Fu  62 b l
Micro Models  46 b r
OMA Office for Metropolitan Architecture  front and back cover, 56–59
P&T Group  60, 61, 144, 145
Pei Partnership Architects  126 b, 127 b l
Rocco Design  8–9, 114–117, 128–131, 168–171
RTKL Associates Inc.  12–13, 132–135
Sasaki Associates Inc.  150–153
Jan Siefke  90, 111 b, 112
SOM Skidmore Owings & Merrill  92–95
Li Wen/Point Studio 148, 149 t
Chaoying Yang  111 t, 113 t, b
Yuanjing Architecture Design Consulting Co. Ltd.  63, 64, 65 t
Yuan Ying  136–139

© Prestel Verlag, Munich · Berlin · London · New York 2005

© for illustrations see Picture Credits p. 191

Front and back cover: CCTV Headquarters, Beijing, OMA Office for Metropolitan Architecture

pp. 4–5: Beijing Capital International Airport, Beijing, Foster and Partners; pp. 6–7: International Automotive Expo, Beijing, Henn Architekten; pp. 8–9: Guangdong Museum, Guangzhou, Rocco Design; pp. 10–11: 2008 Olympics Wukesong Cultural and Sports Center, Beijing, Burckhardt + Partner; pp. 12–13: Chinese Museum of Film, Beijing, RTKL Associates

Prestel Verlag
Königinstrasse 9
80539 Munich
Tel. +49 (89) 38 17 09-0
Fax +49 (89) 38 17 09-35
www.prestel.de

Prestel Publishing Ltd.
4, Bloomsbury Place
London WC1A 2QA
Tel. +44 (20) 73 23-5004
Fax +44 (20) 76 36-8004

Prestel Publishing
900 Broadway, Suite 603
New York, NY 10003
Tel. +1 (212) 995-2720
Fax +1 (212) 995-2733
www.prestel.com

Library of Congress Control Number: 2005904465

British Library Cataloguing-in-Publication Data: a catalogue record for this book is available from the British Library

The Deutsche Bibliothek holds a record of this publication in the Deutsche Nationalbibliografie; detailed bibliographical data can be found under http://dnb.ddb.de

Prestel books are available worldwide. Please contact your nearest bookseller or one of the above addresses for information concerning your local distributor.

Editorial direction: Angeli Sachs, Sandra Leitte
Copyediting: Christopher Wynne
Editorial assistance: Julia Winter

Design, layout and typesetting: WIGEL, Munich
Origination: ReproLine Genceller, Munich
Printing and binding: sellier, Freising

Printed in Germany on acid-free paper

ISBN 3-7913-3270-8